ART STARTS

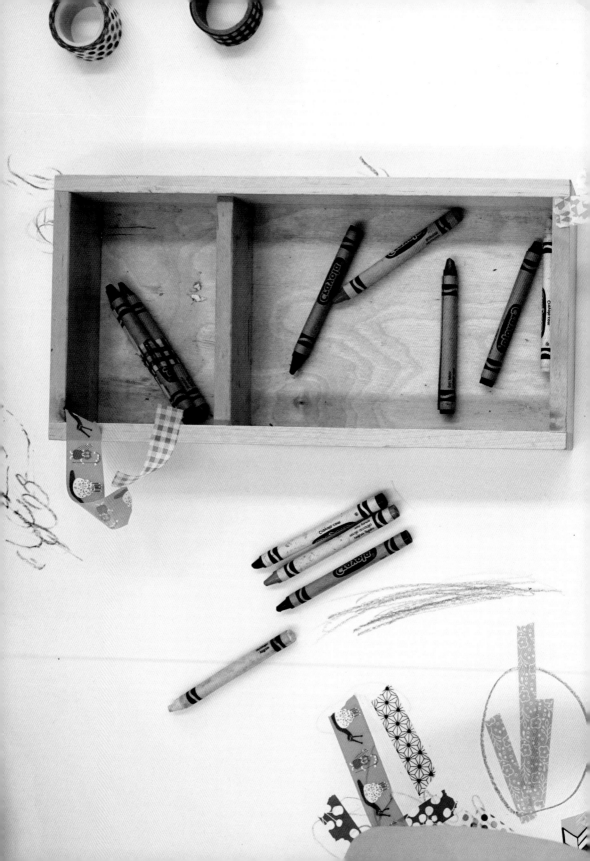

TINKERLAB

ART STARTS

52 PROJECTS
FOR OPEN-ENDED
EXPLORATION

RACHELLE DOORLEY

R⋮
ROOST BOOKS

Roost Books
An imprint of Shambhala Publications, Inc.
4720 Walnut Street
Boulder, Colorado 80301
roostbooks.com

Cover art: Rachelle Doorley
Cover and interior design: Debbie Berne

9 8 7 6 5 4 3 2 1

First Edition
Printed in China

Library of Congress
Cataloging-in-Publication Data

Names: Doorley, Rachelle, author.
Title: TinkerLab art starts: 52 projects for
    open-ended exploration / Rachelle
    Doorley.
Description: Boulder: Roost Books, 2020. |
    Includes bibliographical references and
    index.
Identifiers: LCCN 2019045894 | ISBN
    9781611806687 (trade paperback)
Subjects: LCSH: Handicraft for children. |
    Creative activities and seat work.
Classification: LCC TT160 .D68 2020 | DDC
    745.5083—dc23
LC record available at https://lccn.loc.
    gov/2019045894

For those who care deeply about nurturing creativity, courage, and curiosity in children (even if it's messy), this book is for you.

CONTENTS

INTRODUCTION

Imagine this: It's an hour before dinner and you're standing in a calm kitchen with an open book while your children actively engage in an independent creative project. They're playful, occupied, and imaginative while you take delight in their focus, calmly prepare dinner, and catch up on a chapter of your book. Maybe this sounds like a fantasy? When I had an afternoon just like this, it felt like a dream—I could almost imagine birds chirping and Snow White herself waltzing past the window!

When my children were preschoolers, afternoons like this were a rarity. Typical instead was a tsunami-style surge of dinner assembly, the sound of my name on repeat, counter wiping, sibling squabbles, whining, and redirecting. In short, the word "calm" wouldn't come close to describing our afternoon routine. So, what was this magical moment, and how did it come to pass in the whirlwind of parenting children under the age of five?

Let me back up to the night before this glorious afternoon.

I wanted to create a new normal for our family that felt more purposeful and had an idea that might capture my kids' imaginations. After my children went to bed, I set up a simple art provocation for them to explore in the morning—a freshly cleared table with two large art trays, each set up with stickers, watercolors, paper, and a jar of water. It didn't take long to set up, and my hope was that it would occupy them for just a few creative minutes when they woke up. The bonus, as I imagined, would be a sense of calm for all of us and maybe even, *cough,*

time for a cup of tea and a chat with my husband while observing a joyful scene at the art table.

The crazy thing is that this actually worked. When the girls woke up, I directed them to the table, and their eyes expanded with delight when they saw the beautiful invitation to create. I proposed they explore the supplies by saying, "I wonder what you can create with these materials." Without my telling them exactly what to do, they got busy attaching stickers to the paper, painting, removing stickers, and adding more paint. Especially wonderful was how this open-ended prompt appealed to both of them, because they could access the materials with their own unique sets of questions and capabilities. While all of this magic took place, my morning took a turn for the better with the hot cup of tea *and* conversation. It's the little things.

Later that day I tried this again during the dreaded "witching hour," that challenging hour or two right before dinner, when young children are hungry, tired, and clamor for extra attention. This time I set up playdough, a cookie sheet, a muffin tin, rolling pins, and cookie cutters and asked, "I wonder what you might make with these supplies?" (a simple twist on the question I had asked that morning). Within minutes they were happily occupied with dough squishing, cookie making, and cake decorating, while I calmly prepared dinner on the other side of the room. While our dinner cooked, they chatted with animation about their cookies and birthday cakes, and I read part of my book to the sound of two preschoolers who were hard at play, solving creative problems.

With this newfound knowledge, I started to experiment with more provocations and was able to recreate that magic again and again.

How is such a simple thing so effective? Well, when I offered my daughters the challenge to play and experiment with art materials on their own, with very little instruction, they became completely engaged in making their own choices, coming up with inventive solutions to problems, and drawing on previous ideas as new solutions emerged. They were empowered to have their own self-created experience.

This enchanting art setup is called an *invitation to create*, and the strategy is easy.

INVITATIONS TO CREATE

An invitation to create is a simple arrangement of art materials or objects that children can freely engage with in an open-ended way. There's no expected outcome, and all ideas and interpretations are welcome. Once the materials are set up, children can play with and manipulate the materials in whatever way they desire. While adults can step in to provide inspiration and ideas on how to use the materials, these activities are primarily child-driven.

At first glance, invitations to create can be deceptively simple and even cast an illusion of happenstance. However, there's purpose behind the basic setups and often much more going on than meets the eye.

Invitations to create enable children to tap into higher-level thinking skills, such as critical thinking, problem-solving, and reflection, because they invite children to bring their own questions and ideas to the art table. In short, these simple activities are game changers—both for simplifying parents' lives and for encouraging exploratory thinking and problem-solving.

When you witness children experience invitations to create, you'll notice them ponder past experiences, plan creative solutions to big problems, and design poetic compositions. Their minds are electric with possibility and potential. These basic art prompts, without all the bells and whistles of a heavily structured step-by-step project, are wildly easy to set up and exactly what preschoolers need to develop imagination and creative thinking skills. And it's just these skills that our children will need to thrive in an ambiguous future.

BENEFITS OF CREATIVE THINKING

In our quickly changing world, we are peppered with an overwhelming amount of information, and it has become more important to nimbly identify multiple solutions to obstacles and less important to discover the one "right" answer. As they navigate this field of unforeseen challenges, children will thrive with the skills of flexibility, creativity,

communication, and curiosity. Toward this end, we are charged with raising children who are comfortable with the unknown and eager to tackle it with problem-solving skills, self-efficacy, and critical thinking. This is where unrestricted creativity comes into play!

When children engage in open-ended art making, they're challenged to ask and answer their own questions, which enables them to follow curiosities and think critically. For example, they may wonder about:

- **How the material works.** "What is this material? It's squishy like playdough, but it's harder to use, and messy. If I poke twigs into it, they stick."

- **What the material can do.** "What will the chalk do when I move it slowly? What if I press hard? I moved it slowly on the paper and it made a bumpy line, and then it broke when I pressed hard."
- **How the material can support their ongoing interests.** "How can these boxes help me tell the story that's in my mind? I'm going to make a tunnel that goes across the ocean!"
- **Stories and memories.** "I'm thinking about a trip to a farm and I'm going to make a picture about that. The stickers will be the animals and I'll draw the barn and my family with markers."

While there are many ways to help children think flexibly, creative art experiences can be a safe place for children to explore their curiosities while developing twenty-first-century skills such as critical thinking, creativity, collaboration, and leadership. The possibilities are endless, giving children unlimited room to question and explore.

Beyond a long-term goal of developing creative thinking skills, there are immediate gains to these invitations to create that you'll witness right off the bat. Invitations to create can connect you as a maker family, help save you money because the supplies may already be on your shelf, free you from planning complicated projects, and help children think imaginatively and independently. Young children gravitate to open-ended (process art) projects because they're developmentally appropriate and fun! As you'll soon experience, these prompts incite the freedom of self-expression, play, and most importantly, joy.

While not overwhelming, these prompts do require a smidge of planning, which I will help you with. The beauty of these setups is that they don't require fancy art training or experience. The only prerequisite is a belief that creative thinking is important to children's growth and well-being.

PROCESS ART

Open-ended art, or process art, celebrates the *process* of making art and leaves room for free choice, exploration, discovery, tinkering, expression, and inquiry. The intention behind these projects lies in the *experience of making* the work, rather than the final outcome. In process art, no two creations are alike, and *the maker* leads the way toward the final product. In process art, everything a child makes is "right."

Process art naturally connects to the innate curiosity of children who are busy exploring the world around them. As they play with crayons, clay, paper, or paint, they instinctively push, stretch, cut, squeeze, scrape, tear, bounce, twist, and otherwise move tools to see what they're capable of. When introduced to new materials, children's minds and bodies are activated into research mode, and like any good researcher, they may be captivated by a question or problem such as "what will happen if I add one more block to this pile?" or "what will happen if I paint over the chalk pastels?"

Adults have a treasury of knowledge based on long lives of trial and error, and we may find it easy to quickly answer these questions for children. However, when children have the opportunity to find the answers for themselves, they test out ideas, make mistakes, solve problems, and ultimately build confidence and learn to trust themselves along the way.

Let's take the paint and chalk pastel example further and see where it might take a young researcher who asked, "What will happen if I paint over the chalk pastels?"

They're sitting at a table with watercolor paint, paper, and chalk pastels and wonder, "What will happen if I paint over the chalk pastels?" Next, they come up with a hypothesis: "I think I'll draw firmly with the pastels and they'll stay in place after I paint over them." Next comes a plan: "I'll draw first and then try to paint over the pastels!" and then the action of executing the plan. Then, the results: "The pastels smeared under the paint, not what I expected." This might be followed by a new question, further data collection, or more trials.

When we give children the opportunity to think like researchers, scientists, and artists, we let them know we trust them and believe in their ability to find answers to their big questions. Not only that, this process is low on pressure, accessible to all, and joy inducing.

Each of the invitations in this book honors the spirit of process over product. You'll notice I don't include "steps," but suggestions for getting started. The projects are jumping-off points and inspiration, with tips to extend and expand the prompts in various directions. Once you get going, the magic that stems from your work space will come from your imagination, your child's ideas, or ensuing questions that beg to be answered.

Maybe the concept of process art sounds good in theory, but you have some reservations. This methodology is new to a lot of us, and I understand your concern! Over the years I've connected with thousands of parents who are eager to support their child's creative growth, which means I have heard *so many* reasons to shy away from open-ended art. Maybe one of these objections resonates with you:

- It's hard to let go of an aesthetically pleasing end product.
- Not knowing the end product makes you feel disorganized.
- This seems too loose, and children need more structure.

- You don't know what you're supposed to do to facilitate the experience.
- Children probably won't learn anything, so maybe it's a waste of time.

If any of these concerns feel familiar, I invite you to read through all the tips (see page 40) and then try a few invitations to create. Once you get a taste for how easy this is, and witness the benefits to your child or students, I promise you'll be hooked. One of my favorite moments is when I hear from parents and educators who embrace the invitation to create ethos and come to witness their *children* setting up their own art projects or invitations to create for siblings or family members on their own. This is our goal, and I want this for you!

I encourage you to give this a try. While it may feel uncomfortable at first, trust that the ease and joy of these invitations will come forth in time.

HOW TO USE
THIS BOOK

The inspiration for this book came as I was writing *TinkerLab: A Hands-On Guide for Little Inventors*. Each project in that book is rich and full of directions and tips to help scaffold understanding with preschool STEAM-based learning. It occurred to me that a similar title with simple, easy-to-visualize prompts for each week of the year would be a useful companion. What I've set out to create here is a book that adults and children can flip through to find a project that sparks the imagination; that parents can use to easily find prompts that match the contents of the pantry; and that teachers can use to develop a yearlong curriculum. In essence, I hope this is a user-friendly guide for everyone—kids, adults, and teachers alike.

While you can certainly read through this book front to back, here are some ways to enjoy it:

- Invite children to flip through the pages and find a prompt that they are interested in. When children are motivated and driven by curiosity, opportunities for learning abound.
- Look at your pantry of supplies and find a prompt to go along with what you already have on hand. You'll find that many of the prompts in this book rely on basic materials that are easy to come by.
- Flip through the pages and find a prompt that excites *you*! In the years I've been teaching parents and teachers about process

art, I've learned that when adults are enthusiastic about the materials, children are quick to pick up on that enthusiasm. It rubs off!

- Pay attention to your child's or students' interests and find prompts that match. When we connect with children's interests, we have a greater chance of capturing their curiosity. For example, if your child is a budding engineer, go directly to the building activities in chapter 4 (page 127). If fire trucks bring joy to your child, consider how you could bring fire trucks into various prompts, such as drawing or painting. The simple invitations offer a lot of room to layer in a personalized plan.
- Connect the invitations to the season. Children pay attention to everything and notice falling leaves, snow, blooming flowers, and holiday decorations. Make any of the prompts more meaningful by relating them to the weather or holidays through color or materials. Look at the "Creating Color Variation" section (page 22) for color suggestions that tie into the seasons.
- Build an art habit by trying one invitation to create each week of the year. When you get to the end of the year, repeat! I can't tell you how many times my kids have repeated projects that they forgot they once tried or wanted to add to with more knowledge.

The projects in this book are designed for a one-to-one home setting but can easily be expanded for larger groups of children in homes, childcare settings, and classrooms by simply scaling the materials up for more children. A group of children can share materials, such as a bowl of

buttons, a jar, or markers. For a successful group project, be sure to have individual materials such as pencils or mounds of clay available for each child to explore independently.

When children come into my studio, I like to tell them that they're free to create with their full imaginations. If I offer markers and they prefer crayons, that's fine. If they want to make a picture of an undersea bat or talking flower, there's room for this. One of the most enjoyable parts of watching children partake in open-ended invitations is getting a peek into their thinking. Invitations to create bring out innate curiosities about the world, from symmetry to patterns to color mixing to narratives. Wherever children take their art, my hope is that this book sparks creative joy for you and them, and that you take note of their ideas as you go.

If you want to get started right away, jump right into the activities beginning on page 43 and choose a prompt that looks like fun. You'll find your way! If you'd like to search by materials, go to page 165. This is a handy resource if you have some supplies and don't want to make a special trip to the store. If you want to be a little more strategic and get prepared, read on to learn how to set up your space, what materials you'll need for the prompts, and how to talk to children throughout the creation process.

THE INVITATION TO CREATE FRAMEWORK

While invitations to create are very simple to set up and there are no step-by-step instructions, this simple four-step method is a helpful framework for arranging a successful art invitation. I landed on the handy acronym EASE, which nicely sums up the spirit of this process:

1. **Establish a "Yes!" Space.** Designate a space that's safe for creating and where you are comfortable saying "yes" to your child's ideas.

2. **Arrange materials.** Clear the table or work area of anything that won't be used in the invitation. Artfully arrange art materials to provoke creative ideas. Limit the choice of materials to just a few items.

3. **Suggest.** Gently motivate children to create with prompts such as "I wonder what you can make with these materials" or "Let's play with these supplies and see what we can create."

4. **Encourage.** Help children investigate, play, and explore by reinforcing their curiosity with warm words, enthusiasm, and an open mind.

With this simple framework, you'll be well on your way to the oversized world of open-ended creative exploration. I promise that once your creative battery is charged with the easy-to-set-up prompts in this book, you'll see a difference in your child's or students' creativity and problem-solving skills. The outcome will be worth the (very small) effort!

Let's dig a little deeper into the EASE framework.

ESTABLISH A "YES!" SPACE

A "yes" space is a judgment-free zone where children can feel comfortable using materials with few restrictions. So, our first job is to set up an area where *you* feel comfortable saying "yes" to your child's creative or spontaneous ideas. If your child's art table is placed over a clean carpet or your grandma's antique dining table doubles as the art table, there's a good chance neither of these will be a "yes" space. On the other hand, if the art table is in a corner of the kitchen, on a washable floor and close to a sink, or if your antique table is covered with a waterproof tablecloth, you may be more inclined to say "yes" to making art.

That's what we're going for!

When her boys were five and seven, my friend Rebecca and her husband lived in a small apartment, and they wanted a creative space for the kids to invent and tinker. Rebecca is an artist and her husband is a musician, so their home was already tight on space with countless instruments and endless art supplies. She explained to me that her sons, prolific makers and artists themselves, had nowhere to set up camp. While they were short on room, she valued creativity and wanted her children to have an area where they could spontaneously create *and*

where their creations wouldn't overtake their home. Her solution was to turn their covered patio, a small outdoor extension off the living room, into a maker zone where her boys were welcome to make all they wanted. This was their "yes" space.

Where will your creative space be? It could be the dining table, a corner of your living room floor, or a kid-sized table in the kitchen. There are so many possibilities. Don't be limited to thinking that your creative space has to be the perfect playroom. Children are happy to make just about anywhere. The only rule is to make it a "yes" space.

Try these on for size or come up with your own version of a "yes" space:

- My entire home is limitless, and my children can create wherever they like.
- The dining room is a "yes" space when we're not eating meals and when the table is covered with a tablecloth.
- The kitchen is our "yes" space because the floors are washable and the sink is in the room.
- The maker station in my classroom is a "yes" space where children are free to create on the designated maker table.

Just remember this: if you're comfortable with kids creating freely in their art zone, they'll be more inclined to unleash their ideas!

While you've likely seen examples of elaborate art studios, creativity can grow in the humblest of rooms. If you have space limitations, know that you're not alone. Countless parents have carved out useful art zones with space constraints. When my kids were preschoolers, my husband and I valued creativity above dinner

AGREEMENT

Before getting started, you may want to establish an art-making agreement. The benefit of going through expectations ahead of time is that it allows you to forecast your needs and promote your art area as a "yes" space so you don't have to step in as a naysayer halfway through an art session. You don't have to use all, or any, of these ideas; choose those that feel right to you.

- Handle our tools with care. *Model this and children will understand. For example, show them how to re-cap a marker or how to gently draw with a pastel so it doesn't break.*

- Put away our materials when the project is done.

- Keep our art materials in the art area.

- Cover the table before making art.

parties, and our dining area became a maker zone where the girls were free to play, make, and experiment. The room was furnished with a small table, a rolling cart of basic supplies, a trash can for easy cleanup, and a nearby shelf with paper that they could access when ideas came to them. The recipe for a functional creative space includes basic supplies, a clear space on which to create, open minds, and curiosity.

A Word on Playclothes

Similar to having a "yes" space, you might want to have children wear playclothes or art cover-ups while creating. Nothing stops a child from feeling free to create like being told to be careful about getting paint or marker on nice clothes. If your child lives in playclothes, this isn't an issue, but if that's not your style, you could keep small aprons handy for creative projects. An adult button-up shirt, worn backward and buttoned in the back, makes an easy makeshift apron that offers great coverage. If children are wearing long sleeves (playclothes or not), I always help them roll up sleeves to avoid dragging them through wet media like paint and glue.

ARRANGE MATERIALS

Now that you've established your "yes" space, let's talk supplies. In this section I'll go over some finer details on materials: a full list of what's covered in the 52 invitations, ideas on how to organize them in your space, and how you can combine them for different effects.

The prompts in this book are organized into four sections by type of material: dry media, wet media, collage, and building. Most of the prompts use fairly simple materials, many of which you likely already have and some that are fun and worth seeking out. Here's an overview

of the basic supplies, plus some extra treasures that can add flair to the usual.

The Basics

If you're *just* getting started, twelve basic materials will get you through many of the projects without buying anything else.

Dry Materials

Drawing is one of the easiest ways to create an image. There are multiple drawing tools beyond crayons and pens. We'll explore a range of media, including oil pastels, chalk pastels, markers, and charcoal, to help push expectations of what can be used for mark making. In this section and the next, you may notice a handful of invitations that focus on circles. This is because children's earliest pictures are often based on circles.

Wet Materials

In this book, wet media refers to thick paint, glue, and watercolors. These projects have the potential to be messy, so you may want to prep the work space with washable paint and a covered table. Wet projects are also happy in outdoor spaces, over uncarpeted floors, and near sinks.

Collage Materials

A collage is made by attaching material to paper or other surfaces with an adhesive like tape or glue. Start a box for your paper collection of newspaper pieces, discarded magazines, and junk mail, and you'll never

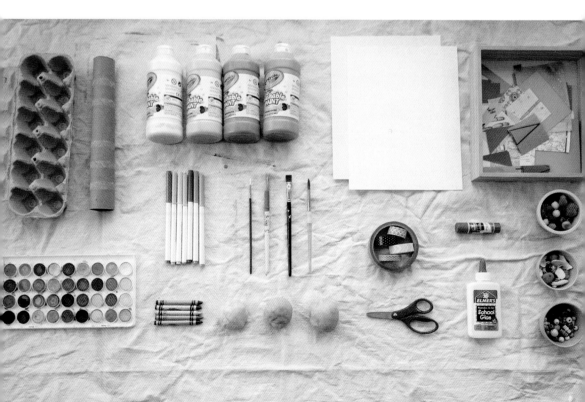

ART MATERIALS

Basic Supplies

If you're just starting out, begin with these basic materials and you'll be ready for many of the invitations in this book.

Crayons. Wax crayons, paint sticks, and gel crayons are all favorites and can be used interchangeably for the projects in this book.

Glue. You'll be glad to have white glue (also called PVA glue) and glue sticks on hand. I like to use washable glue when possible. For little hands, I like to squeeze glue into a jar and add a sturdy paintbrush for easy gluing. I also recommend a low-heat glue gun as an invaluable tool for efficient building with recycled materials such as cardboard.

Markers. Thick and thin, washable markers are my favorite. Store these horizontally or tip down to keep them from drying out quickly.

Paintbrushes. Look for stiff-bristled brushes to use with glue and tempera poster paint and softer watercolor paintbrushes to use with watercolors. I like to encourage kids to experiment with paintbrushes, and a variety pack of brushes is a worthwhile investment.

Paper. Collect all sorts of paper: drawing paper, watercolor paper, copy paper, construction paper, and paper scraps. Oversized paper is especially appealing to young children who aren't proficient with small motor activities and naturally move their arms in large sweeping movements. Many of the "wet material" invitations in this book mention heavy paper, which could be any paper that's at least 50 pounds. Thinner paper will work too, but you may notice it buckles when wet. Watercolor paper and cardstock paper are two examples that will work for prompts that call for *heavy paper*. Fill a box with paper scraps of wrapping paper, postcards, and magazine cutouts to use with collages.

Playdough. Homemade playdough is the best because it's easy to make, economical, and you'll know exactly what ingredients go into it. See page 157 for directions on how to make your own.

Recyclables. We'll use these for collage and building projects. Save materials such as cardboard, paper towel tubes, egg cartons, junk mail, and magazines.

Scissors. Blunt tip or pointed tip kid scissors are a safe bet. If your child is left-handed, look for left-handed scissors.

Tape. Painter's tape is useful for taping paper down to a table and masking off a border or shapes before painting. Decorative tape (aka washi tape) comes in a variety of patterns and is an intriguing option for collage projects.

Tempera poster paint. This thick paint is the consistency of yogurt and usually comes in a bottle. It's great for covering large surfaces, and if you find the washable type, they won't stain clothes. Squeeze each in a jar, add a brush, and take them to the easel.

Treasures. This could be any small, delightful material such as pom-poms, feathers, leaves, craft sticks, or pine cones that kids can add to collages or building projects.

Watercolor paint. I recommend two different kinds of watercolors: First, find the dry paint that comes in oval shapes in a pan. Second, and a little more difficult to come by but worth the effort, look for a set of liquid watercolors. Liquid watercolors are the consistency of food coloring (a fine substitute). They can be used in paint projects and also added to color homemade playdough.

be lacking material with which to collage. In addition to paper, we'll collage with fiber materials such as yarn and fabric, and small treasures such as beads or feathers, so keep an eye out for anything that can be glued to a flat surface.

Building Materials

I've worked with many children who adore creating but can't find their groove with two-dimensional art. However, when faced with three-dimensional forms, a world of possibility opens, which is why this section is so important. All kids should have the opportunity to create in 3-D, and some kids really, really love it. We'll explore squishy clay, dough, recycled materials, tape, glue, wood, and string.

Creating Color Variation

An easy way to change up an invitation is to make variations based on the seasons or colors. Use paper, pens, or paint in these color combinations to coordinate with the time of year, making relevant and meaningful connections for your child or students:

- Red + orange + yellow + green = autumn
- Blues + white = winter, snow, Hanukkah
- Red + green + white = Christmas (Be careful here because mixing red + green paint = brown.)
- Red + white = Valentine's Day
- Shades of green = St. Patrick's Day, spring, Earth Day
- Pastels in pink + yellow + green + lavender = spring, Easter, Mother's Day
- Red + white + blue = Independence Day, Memorial Day

COMPREHENSIVE SUPPLY LIST

If you'd like to see all the supplies included in this book, this is your comprehensive material list for the projects, grouped by the section where you'll find them in the store.

Paper
Bleeding tissue paper
Cardboard
Construction paper—both colorful and black
Copy paper
Drawing paper
Heavy paper: 50 lb. or heavier, such as cardstock, water-color, art paper, or sulphite
Large-sheet paper, such as a paper roll or grocery bags taped together
Origami or colored copy paper
Paper scraps
Tissue paper
Watercolor paper

Paint
Liquid watercolor or food coloring
Tempera cake paint
Tempera poster paint: various colors, black, and white
Watercolor paint

Glue/Tape
Decorative tape
Glue stick
Low-temperature glue gun and glue sticks
Painter's Tape
Small glue bottles
White glue

Drawing Tools
Chalk pastels (or col-ored chalk)
Colored pencils
Compressed charcoal
Crayons
Dot (bingo) markers
Oil pastels
Markers
Pencils
Permanent markers
Stencil paintbrushes (aka dabber)

Sturdy paintbrushes
Tempera paint sticks or gel crayons
Unwrapped crayons
Watercolor paintbrushes

Fiber
Burlap or other large-weave fabric
Colored felt
Darning needle or other blunt needle with a large eye
Embroidery hoop
Fabric scraps
String
White felt, roughly 12" × 18" (30 × 46 cm)
Yarn—various colors

Tools
Adult and child scissors
Black-and-white photo with extra white space (see pages 158–61)
Eye stickers
Hole punchers
Kneaded charcoal eraser
Paper punchers
Stapler
Stencils
Wire cutters

Household Items
Baking tray
Blocks
Cardboard egg carton
Cardboard towel tubes
Clear vinyl contact paper
Comb
Containers to hold tempera paint
Cookie cutters
Cotton swabs
Cups, lids, paper towel tubes, and other round printing objects

Fork
Jar for water
Muffin tin
Old credit card or small pieces of cardboard
Paper plate
Paper towels or round coffee filters
Party tray
Pipette or eyedropper
Plates to hold paint
Potato masher
Rolling pin
Skewers
Small bowls
Small flowerpot
Small rag
Sponges
Straws
Thin wire—24 gauge floral wire is easy to work with
Toothpicks
Vase of flowers

Treasures
Beads
Beads with large holes
Buttons
Circle stickers
Corks
Craft sticks
Feathers
Pipe cleaners
Pom-poms
Plain wood beads
Sequins
Stickers

Nature Items
Fresh leaves
Nature objects, such as pine cones and seashells
Twigs
Water
Wood pieces

Clay
Air-dry clay
Modeling clay
Playdough (see page 157)

- Black + red + green = Kwanzaa
- Orange + black = Halloween

Another way to achieve color variety and harmony is to create a color family by including colors that are all warm, all cool, all neutral, or all shades of one color. Here are some examples:

- Reds + pinks (shades of one color)
- Yellows + greens (analogous colors)
- Whites + beige + tan (neutral colors)

Organizing Your Supplies

Once you've staked out your "yes" space and gathered your supplies, it's time to organize everything. Friends, save your sanity and keep it simple! I've talked to countless parents who lament over their disorganized art spaces, and I don't want you to sweat this. If your space isn't picture perfect, guess what? Your child will not be concerned! If you have materials and a place to store them, you're good to go!

That said, there are so many ways to do this, depending on budget, intention, and the space itself. While we each have different ideas about organization, and what works for one won't necessarily work for another, here are a few tips that I've learned over the years from my experience in the classroom, in workshops, in my own home, and from other parents and educators:

- **Open shelves** help children easily see the materials they're looking for without too much friction. You know the old saying

"Out of sight, out of mind"? If you want children to use art materials, do your best to keep them visible.

Don't put anything on the shelves that you're not comfortable giving children free access to! For example, permanent markers or bottles of paint might cause you some concern with toddlers. Understandable. Store these away and only bring them out when you can supervise.

Related, if you have toddlers *and* older children, move everything out of your toddler's reach until they're old enough to safely access supplies. You know your children best, but this has always served me well.

- **Rolling carts** are useful for moving art supplies to various places in a room, and also for creating an instant art zone in the absence of shelves.
- Store supplies in **clear containers**, such as plastic shoeboxes and mason jars. This will help you (and children) find the supplies you're looking for and make cleanup easier. You could even go the extra mile and label these or add picture labels of what's inside.
- **Trays and baskets** are lovely for holding paper, paper scraps, and larger items.
- **Small bowls** are great for holding the supplies for specific invitations to create.
- Store **paintbrushes** upright in jars.
- Store **felt markers** in jars with the capped tips facing down, to keep the ink in the nibs. I always forget this and store mine the other way around, and then wonder why my pens dry out.
- **Baking trays** are useful for presenting invitations that are on the drippy side. The tray will do wonders for keeping liquids in one spot.
- Keep **towels and a trash can** in the maker area for quick cleanup. I promise, this will give you peace of mind.

It doesn't take a lot to set up a creative space. Start with a shelf, bookcase, or rolling cart and fill it up with basic supplies, and you'll be well equipped to put together invitations to create for your child or students. Begin small, iterate as children grow, and give yourself grace if things feel more chaotic than you'd like. It will all come together in time.

SETTING UP INVITATIONS

Now for the fun part! It's time to set up an invitation to create.

First, think of the invitations in this book as inspiration to get you started. If you don't have exactly what you see in the photos or supply lists, feel free to substitute with different materials. I do this all the time, and often this flexibility and resourcefulness leads me to even better ideas. If you happen upon a fabulous twist on one of the invitations in this book, please reach out and tell me about it!

Second, since we're in the business of making art, aesthetics are understandably important. People are attracted to things that look nice, and if you arrange an attractive invitation, it's more likely your child will want to explore what's offered. Please don't go overboard, but do what you can to clear away distractions and create a pleasing invitation that draws your child in.

While setting up an invitation is simple, it's helpful to do so with some intention and care. Here are some tips for doing just that.

Work Area. First, clear off the table. It's always inspiring to start with a clean slate.

Trays. Trays are a useful tool for organizing invitations ahead of time as well as for presenting some invitations. If you want to plan ahead, lay out all the materials for the invitation on the tray the night before, and then simply pull out the tray the next day, ready to go! Trays are also a convenient way to contain the mess of doughs and liquid paints. Trays with high edges can inhibit arm movements while kids are creating, and if you notice this, just remove the tray from the table.

Tape the Paper Down. To save the frustration of paper slipping around while painting, you may want to tape the edges of the paper down for your littlest makers. Older children often like the flexibility of moving their paper while they work.

Bowls and Baskets. Present art materials in shallow bowls and baskets. Try to use neutral containers so that the materials take center stage.

Mark-Making Tools. Select *a few* mark-making tools—not too many—and place them on the table or in a container. This helps avoid overwhelm. If children want to gather more supplies once the project is underway, that's totally fine.

Paper Selection. Have a variety of paper for different art-making purposes and experiments. Construction paper is slightly textured and works well with chalk and oil pastels. Copy paper is great for markers, crayons, pencils, and everyday drawing. Many of the "wet materials" invitations in this book use heavy paper, which could be any paper that's at least 50 pounds, such as watercolor paper or cardstock paper. Thinner paper will work too, but you may notice it buckles when wet.

Painting. For successful painting invitations, here are some tried and tested strategies:

- Look for "stackable wide-base no-tip water pots." These are amazing, especially for toddlers and preschoolers.

- You'll see a lot of mason jars in this book. While they're glass, I have yet to experience a problem with them. Half-fill the 16-ounce jars with water for paintbrush cleaning. Kids like to see the water change colors while cleaning.
- Have a collection of thick, medium, and thin paintbrushes for paint exploration, experiments, and detail work.
- Place a rag in the painting area for drying off paintbrushes between colors.
- To clean the paintbrush, dance it up and down in the water, and then wipe it on a rag to dry it off.
- Avoid leaving paintbrushes in water for long stretches of time as it can damage the bristles.

When to Set Up Invitations to Create

There really isn't a bad time for an invitation to create, but there are a few times that have worked well for me and for the parents that I work with. When my kids were one and three, I liked to set these up during my baby's nap, so I could have quality time with my older child. When my girls were five and seven, I would get these together at night for them to explore on their own in the morning. Older children who get the hang of invitations will enjoy the challenge of setting up prompts with you. I've had a number of parents report that once their children became comfortable with the routine of invitations, they would independently set up their own versions of the prompts for their family and friends! Try one or all of these times and see what works for you.

Early Morning. Set up the invitation at night, after your child has gone to bed, so that it's ready first thing in the morning.

Afternoon. Set up the invitation to create during a nap so that your child wakes up to an art invitation.

During a Sibling's Nap. If you have children of different ages, such as a toddler and a five-year-old, set up an invitation to create for your older child while the toddler naps. This is great for one-on-one time and allows your older child to explore at their level undistracted.

Late Afternoon. Arrange a simple, not too messy prompt that doesn't require a lot of supervision so that you can get dinner ready and unwind. You can also have your child help you set up the art prompt to build agency!

At School. If you're a teacher, try one of these ideas: set up a prompt for your students to explore each day in an art learning station; have a material theme for the week, such as "clay," and invite the children to explore clay with different tools; or set up an invitation for early finishers to work on quietly.

There's really not a bad time to create an invitation. If the mood strikes or if you have a few minutes to spare, set one up and see what happens.

How to Clean Up an Art Session

One of the most common hurdles to setting up art prompts is the potential mess of creating—dirty floors, paint on the table, and accumulated projects with no extra storage in sight. These are all real challenges, and I'm not going to say they aren't part of the deal. So yes, the mess is real, we can't change that, but we can work on how we *think* about messes and how we *handle* messes.

As for how we *think* about messes, let's use cooking as a metaphor. When we're hungry for dinner, we pull out ingredients, chop them, cook them, assemble them, set a table, and then eat them. In the process we've likely created a mess of knives, boards, pans, dishes, and flatware. Cleaning up is no simple task, but we've accepted that it's part of the deal if we want to eat. Likewise, if we want to fuel our creative minds, it's helpful to acknowledge that art prep and cleanup are part of the deal. While it may not be fun, it's easier to swallow if we remember we're filling our creative well.

That said, enlisting kids to help with cleanup is key to your success. Not only will this help you, it will give children important skills in responsibility and follow-through. For handling the mess, these are my favorite tricks.

Establish Guidelines. Kids don't know what they don't know! Lay down all the rules before you get started so they have a clear understanding of your expectations. See the art-making agreement sidebar on page 17 for more on this.

Cover the Table. If you don't have a table that can take a beating, cover the table with a vinyl tablecloth (look for oilcloth at the hardware store), shower curtain, newspaper, kraft paper, or a canvas drop cloth that's designed for house painting.

Work over a Washable Floor. Carpets and art are not the best of friends. If you have a carpet in your art area, lay down a tarp so you don't have a panic attack every time the playdough comes out. Kitchen and wood floors, however, are great for family maker spaces.

Buy Washable. When buying art supplies, and especially paint, look for "washable" on the label.

Set Up Tidying Tools. Keep a trash can in your maker space and a broom and dustpan nearby for sweeping up scraps.

Store Materials in Clear Containers. This will help children see where tools and supplies go when the creative session is over.

Keep Towels and Water on Hand. When working with wet materials (paint—eek!), have simple supplies such as wet rags, paper towels, or baby wipes handy for quick cleanup tasks.

Keep Messy Hands Together. If messy hands have to make their way to a sink, have children hold their hands together on the way there. This will help keep hands from hitting walls along the way.

Many Hands Make Light Work. Invite children to help clean up. If you haven't already tried this, you may be surprised that they actually like cleaning. Favorite tasks include wiping down the table with a damp sponge, putting scraps in the wastebasket, and putting jars back on the shelf. Young kids generally enjoy being part of the cleanup process, so starting this at an early age is key to keeping it going in the years to come.

SUGGEST

Now that the invitation to create is set up, you may wonder about *your* role while your child or student creates. How do you motivate your child to get started, how much do you get involved, and what do you say along the way to encourage creativity and exploration?

First, motivation! Generating enthusiasm for making is often as simple as using warm words that encourage children to experiment, iterate, and explore. Begin by inviting children to the prompt with a suggestion like, "I wonder what we can create with these materials?" This question works because it doesn't suggest a specific outcome and it activates your child's mind with possibilities.

I like to use these three magical starters to catalyze ideas: "I wonder . . ." "Let's see what . . ." and "How could we . . . ?"

For example:

- I wonder what you can make with these supplies?
- Let's see what we can create with markers and paper.
- How could we use these materials to make something for each other?

Try them and see if they work for you, too.

Once children are engaged in making, I'm often asked how much assistance adults should give them. If your child asks for help with something they're struggling with, a constructive strategy is to help them brainstorm possible solutions. To do this, discuss what they're trying to accomplish and see if you can help break down the goal into steps. From there you can encourage experimentation with different solutions, or try modeling ideas for your child on your own piece of paper.

Sometimes children who ask for help struggle with perfectionism. When this comes up, you can model how it's okay to make mistakes, play, and experiment. I can't emphasize the importance of encouraging experimentation enough! To do this, set up your own art supplies, talk through the challenges of the materials, play with them, express the mistakes you're making, and come up with solutions along the way. Demonstrating your willingness to make mistakes and recover from them can help your child develop their own growth mind-set.

I've talked to countless adults who share how their childhood creativity was silenced by an adult (sometimes well meaning, sometimes not) who drew on their work or told them how to make their work better. When a child has an experience like this, it can make them feel vulnerable or anxious about continuing. When your child asks for help, notice any urge to "fix" their art. Don't draw directly on a child's work or make design choices for a child. I really can't stress this enough. Children need room to muddle through creative decisions as well as time to test out their own ideas. The process of experimentation, however difficult it may seem in the short run, will give your child tools of creative courage and self-efficacy.

As children get absorbed by the creation process, you may observe deep focus. In these moments, children don't need to be interrupted with questions or comments. Simply give them room to explore and then follow up with an invitation to reflect together. If you talk to children during the process, try to keep comments objective and avoid making comments that indicate any bias, preferences, or opinions about the work.

Sometimes kids are slow to warm to an invitation. That's okay! It can happen for a number of reasons. It could be that they're not in the mood to create, they're not interested in the prompt or supplies, something else has their attention, or they have their own ideas. Just roll with it and follow their interests. Our primary goal is to encourage creative thinking, and forcing the point won't help.

I have a few tricks that you can try, however, to get the ball rolling: If children are hesitant to jump in, show your enthusiasm for the materials by giving the prompt a try. The simple act of being a role model can go a long way toward building children's curiosity. Maybe the materials aren't exciting, in which case you can ask your child or students if they'd like to add another material to the table. If you think they're distracted by other (better!) options, simply bring out the invitation another time. I once had a parent tell me her child wasn't interested in the invitation she set up and that perhaps it was because the family got a new puppy the day before. Yep, that will do it!

The beautiful thing about these invitations is that they will meet every child exactly where they may be. Some children enjoy making abstract images and others gravitate toward realism. Some work slowly and others fast. Some take delight in paint and others in drawing. As your child creates, take note of what you observe. If they like to tell stories about their art, you can write these down on sticky notes and later attach them to the back of the work as a memory keeper.

Providing the space for your child to make creative choices with confidence will reward you with a better understanding of what drives their curiosity and imagination. Pay attention to what materials they gravitate to, notice what they're curious about (this is the most fun part, in my opinion), take note of the comments and questions that come up, and then make adjustments for future projects. Children will find meaning in tailored experiences that account for their curiosity.

ENCOURAGE

In this section we'll discuss how to help children investigate, play, and explore by reinforcing their curiosity with warm words, enthusiasm, and an open mind.

Talking with Children about Their Art

The language we use can play a big role in how children see themselves as makers and view their creative role in the world.

- Ask open-ended questions. When asking children about their art, inquire with open-ended questions that demonstrate authentic curiosity in the absence of judgment. For example, "can you tell me more about how you made this?" is nicer to hear than a close-ended question such as "did you make a car?"

- Make observational comments. Sometimes children will ask you if you like what they made. By all means answer "yes," but don't get too carried away with superlatives that may lead them to create art as a way of seeking praise. A good practice is to state what you notice, such as "I see you attached the paper to the wood with tape" or "I noticed that you spent a lot of time working on this area." This approach comes from a place of curiosity and shows makers that you're paying attention to their ideas and effort. It also signals to children that they can make for the sake of making and that there isn't a right or wrong way to create.

- When you present a prompt, simply say, "I wonder what you can create with these materials." If you plan to join your child or students, you could say, "I wonder what *we* can make with these materials."

- If children are lost in thought, try to hold back from commenting on art making *during* the art process. When makers are in the flow of creativity, talking to them can be distracting and stop that flow.

- Some children like to talk while they create, so don't hold back from conversation if it feels like they would prefer this.

- Keep comments factual and avoid saying anything subjective or opinion-based that focuses on the final product. While opinions are usually shared with good intentions, when children hear that you "like" their work or that you think it's "pretty," they may hear your bias and be inclined to make more work that pleases you rather than create things that stem from their own ideas and imagination. A factual comment is "I saw that you mixed red and yellow paint." An opinion comment is "I like that rainbow; it's pretty."

- If you want to be encouraging, comment on the process or your child's effort by saying something like, "I noticed that you worked hard on this."
- If you make art alongside your child or students, be playful, acknowledge and incorporate their excellent ideas into your work, acknowledge your mistakes (kids love seeing grown-ups fumble through problems and then resolve them), and allow your work to be imperfect.
- Comment on what you observed during children's creative practice as a way to help build a more complex art vocabulary. For example, "I noticed that you moved the paintbrush in *vertical lines* across the paper" or "Can you tell me how you *blended* the *charcoal* in this area?"

Questions while Creating

Making art alongside your child is a great opportunity to connect, build vocabulary, and hear your child's ideas. Here are some ideas for questions you can ask during an art session:

- Sensory: What does the paint feel like on your hands? What sounds does the clay make when you squish it? How does the pastel move on the paper?
- Materials: What materials do you see on the table? What do you notice about them? How does the paintbrush move? How could we get these beads on the yarn?

- Communication: How can you use the paint to make a story about our trip to the beach? How can you use charcoal to make a portrait of our dog?

Questions about Process

Talking about art can help you and your child to solidify concepts and learning, build vocabulary, make abstract connections, and relate with one another. Once children have completed their work, it can be enjoyable and illuminating to discover what they had in mind. Ask them to tell you about what they created and how they made it. Young children often have an easier time talking about *how* they made something or *what story* they created than talking about the intention or idea behind a piece.

Questions should be open-ended and focus on process rather than product. Here are some examples:

- What can you tell me about your picture?
- Can you tell me how you made this area (pointing to the area)?
- I heard you talking about a story when you were making this. Can you tell me more about what's happening in the picture?
- I saw you mixing colors in this area (pointing to it). Can you tell me how you did that?
- It looked like you had a lot of fun making this. Can you share more about how you made it?

Taking this one step further, you may want to write some of these stories or direct quotes on the back of the artwork so that you or the child can remember the context in the years to come.

Tips for a Successful Creative Session

Once you get rolling with invitations to create, questions are sure to pop up around what children are experiencing and how to extend the learning beyond these prompts. Here are a few thoughts based on conversations I've had with parents over the years.

It's OK to Model How to Use a New Material. Though the prompts can be used with little instruction, sometimes children need guidance. While modeling how materials work or could be used is OK, making art *for* children or drawing on children's art is counterproductive. Always demonstrate on your own work in the spirit of experimentation.

Look for Opportunities to Extend Learning. As you observe how children react to an invitation, take note of what's interesting to them, what questions they ask, and what they find challenging. As you reflect, consider how you could extend the prompt from a spark into another provocation.

Process and Product Are Interconnected. It's okay if children are product-oriented. While the invitations in this book are process-based, it's important to remember that even our youngest makers who are instinctively driven to create freely often have a specific outcome in mind while they create. It may not be evident to us because children can't always articulate their plans, but goals and intentions can drive their curiosity. That drive could be a goal to mix colors, test how a paintbrush works, or discover what happens when you stack just one more block on top of the tower. These goals are the child's equivalent of product.

Deep Work and Repetition Build Confidence and Understanding. It's through repetition that children begin to recognize patterns and feel more comfortable experimenting and iterating. If your child or students adore one of the prompts in this book, they may want to try it again. You can add different colors or slightly different materials. In our home, we repeat projects constantly, and often make them more complex as the kids get older.

Congratulations! You made it this far, which means you're officially ready to set up an invitation to create. Where to begin? Flip through the next four sections, find something that catches your eye, and start there. If you don't have many materials yet, don't let that stop you. When my oldest daughter was sixteen months, I was eager to create art with her, but all I had were a few crayons and a roll of paper. Guess what? We rocked that roll of paper and crayons for months before moving on to different materials. While some of the setups in this book require a trip to the art store, most are basic. These three provocations are possible with just paper, pens, and glue: Connect the Dots on page 45, Fill-a-Frame on page 53, or Collage Buffet on page 111.

When you spark creativity in the little people in your life, you'll be rewarded by what emerges, I promise. And if Snow White happens to waltz by your window one morning while your children are deeply engaged in creative play, please drop me a line to tell me about it!

Nothing is a mistake. There's no win and no fail. There's only make.

—Sister Corita Kent,
art activist, college art educator

PART 1

CRAYONS, PAPER, STICKERS,

AND OTHER DRY MATERIALS

"Mama, I covered all the dots!"—Tate

TINKERLAB ART STARTS

# CONNECT THE DOTS

● **Drawing paper** ● **Oil pastels**

Draw dots all over a sheet of paper. Invite your child to connect the dots into shapes, real or imagined. Color the shapes in and add details.

VARIATIONS

Try this with markers, crayons, or colored pencils.

Invite your child to make a page of dots for you.

Work collaboratively (on the same sheet) and take turns finding and making shapes.

Tell a story based on the shapes that emerge.

TINKERLAB ART STARTS

② CRAYONS AND TAPE

- Child scissors
- Crayons
- Decorative tape
- Drawing paper

Cover a table with paper. Place crayons, tape, and scissors on the table. Invite your child to create.

TIPS

For younger children, precut the tape into small pieces and attach them to a wooden block or something similar.

A wide variety of tape options can make this prompt extra exciting.

VARIATION

Bundle a group of three crayons together with tape or rubber bands and invite your child to draw with this super-crayon.

"Firemen are putting out a fire. I'm really grateful for firemen. Charcoal is messy. I liked rubbing it and making the smoke."–Emeline

③ CHARCOAL MARKS

- Compressed charcoal
- Kneaded charcoal eraser
- Painter's tape
- Paper with texture, such as watercolor or construction paper
- Small rag

Tape the edges of the paper to the table so it won't wiggle while your child creates. Demonstrate how to use the tip and the edge of the charcoal for different effects. Invite your child to draw with the charcoal. Use the rag to blend the charcoal and use the eraser to remove it.

VARIATIONS

Alongside the charcoal, offer white chalk pastel for adding highlights.

Experiment with pressure (pressing light and hard), blending charcoal with fingers, rubbing the side of the charcoal on the paper, or using papers of different textures (smooth, coarse).

TIPS

Break the charcoal into shorter pieces for small hands.

Charcoal can be messy, so cover your table with a cloth to collect dust.

If your child doesn't like the feeling of charcoal, you can wrap a tissue around the end of it to keep fingers cleaner.

Have a damp rag ready to wipe dusty hands.

TINKERLAB ART STARTS

 CIRCLE DRAWINGS

- Drawing paper
- Markers

Prepare the paper by drawing a grid of circles. Invite your child to fill in the circles with designs or pictures.

TIP

Use the end of a paper towel tube dipped in paint to stamp circles on paper, then allow to dry for about an hour. You can also trace a cup, use a compass, or draw freehand.

VARIATIONS

Working side by side, collaborate by taking turns filling in the circles.

Leave some space around the circles for adding other ideas to the background.

"I was going to make an ocean in the square, and then I realized I could make a nautilus, and I drew an underwater bat."–Nirvan

 ⑤ FILL-A-FRAME

● **Drawing paper**   ● **Markers**

Draw a series of frames on a sheet of paper or photocopy the frames on pages 162–63. Invite your child to fill in the frames with pictures.

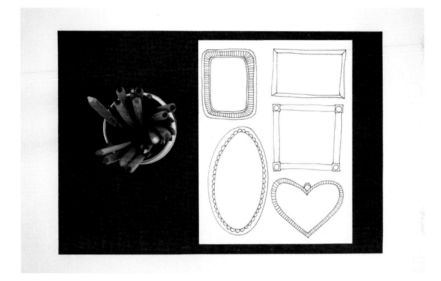

VARIATIONS

Display the finished project by cutting the frames out and attaching them to a wall.

Go big and draw frames on an oversized sheet of paper or a large roll of paper that rolls out on the ground or attaches to a wall.

Make photocopies of your frame page to bring on trips.

Think of the frames as a comic and fill them with scenes from a story.

TINKERLAB ART STARTS

 CHALK PASTELS

- Chalk pastels
- Construction paper, any color
- Water, in bowl

Set up the chalk pastels and paper. Invite your child to draw with the pastels. Once this runs its course, offer a bowl of water in addition to the other materials. Invite your child to dip the chalk in water before drawing. What happens?

TIPS

This prompt works best on paper that has some texture to it.

Some children won't like the dry texture of chalk and will benefit from wrapping an end of the chalk with a tissue to hold it.

VARIATIONS

Offer a small rag for color blending.

Draw with chalk on superfine sandpaper (300 grit or higher) for a vibrant effect.

Set up a variety of natural objects, such as seashells or leaves, and invite your child to draw what they see.

Offer white chalk and black construction paper for an exploration of high contrast with black and white.

"I like feeling the leaf first and then seeing how the texture comes up on the paper. It wasn't that difficult for me. I liked painting because it looked like a leaf in a color."–Charlotte

⑦ LEAF RUBBING

● **Copy paper** ● **Crayons** ● **Fresh leaves**

Unwrap a few crayons and break them in half. Set them up with leaves and paper. Invite your child to place a leaf beneath the paper and then rub the side of a crayon over the leaf. The outline and veins of the leaf will transfer to the paper.

TIP

Dry leaves can fall apart and may not work as well for this prompt.

VARIATIONS

Before beginning this project, make an activity out of collecting fresh leaves.

Use more than one crayon color.

When your child is done, invite them to paint over the leaf rubbing with watercolors. The crayon will resist the watercolors and show through the paint.

"It's nighttime. It's a slide that goes into the pool."-Genevieve

8 OIL PASTEL ON BLACK PAPER

- **Black construction paper**
- **Oil pastels**

Invite your child to draw on the paper with oil pastels. Oil pastels, a creamier version of crayons, blend easily and make marks with little effort.

TIP

A heavy, textured paper such as construction paper or watercolor paper works best for this prompt.

VARIATIONS

Offer a cup of oil and cotton swabs alongside the pastels. Invite your child to dip the cotton swabs in the oil and use them to blend the colors directly on the paper.

Try this with different colors of paper.

"This is a crab with twenty-two eyeballs. Eye stickers are fun because you don't have to draw all those eyes."–Kai

9 EYE SEE YOU

- **Drawing paper**
- **Eye stickers**
- **Markers**

Attach eye stickers to the paper. Invite your child to add features around the eyes to make animals, people, insects, or even imaginary creatures.

VARIATIONS

If you don't have eye stickers, simply draw eyes on the paper.

Place a few sets of eyes on the paper to indicate the possibility of a family, zoo, or flock of birds.

To further stoke the imagination, in addition to eyes, draw a few basic details, such as cat whiskers or bunny ears.

Try this with colored pencils or crayons.

Offer your child a few eye stickers to place on the paper.

"I like drawing. I drew Batman."-Taisen
"I drew a dinosaur on all the pages."-Lucy

⑩ BOOK MAKING

- Colored pencils
- Colorful paper (one sheet)
- Copy paper (three sheets)
- Paper punchers
- Stapler
- Stencils
- Stickers
- Tempera paint stick or gel crayons

Form the sheets of paper into a stack, with the colorful paper on top, and fold the stack in half. Secure the paper into a book by stapling the creased side in two places. Invite your child to make a book with tools provided.

VARIATIONS

Make a book with lightweight watercolor paper and offer your child watercolors to paint the pages.

Make an assortment of books in different sizes and see which one your child gravitates to.

Write a book together.

Offer additional collage materials such as glue and construction paper.

Make a nature journal. Take your book on a walk and document what you see along the way.

No stapler? Punch two holes along the spine and connect the holes with ribbon.

"This is me and my cat jumping on a big, giant flower."—Theodore

TINKERLAB ART STARTS

⑪ FLOWER DRAWING

- Drawing paper
- Tempera paint stick or gel crayons

- Vase of flowers

Set up a vase or pot of flowers. Place paint sticks and paper on the table. Invite your child to draw.

VARIATIONS

Take paper, colored pencils, a clipboard, and a magnifying glass outdoors for plein air drawing; you can carry these supplies in a backpack for breaks on nature hikes.

Draw a frame on the paper to fill in with what they see (see Fill-a-Frame, page 53).

Invite your child to draw with permanent marker and then paint it in with watercolors.

Make this seasonal by setting up a simple still life from seasonal objects such as gourds and apples in fall, flowers in spring, fruit and seashells in summer, or candy canes and holly in winter.

TIP

Allow children to draw anything they like. They may be inspired by the flowers, something else in the room, a memory, or ideas from their imagination.

"I liked using a realistic picture that you can add to, and then adding my own drawing made it all look good together."—Madeline

12 BLACK-AND-WHITE PHOTO STARTER

- **Black-and-white photo with extra white space (pages 158–61)**
- **Colored pencils**
- **Markers**

Find a black-and-white photo of a car, tree, house, toy, or other object that appeals to your child's interests. Print the image and place it on the table next to the drawing tools. Invite your child to draw.

TIPS

If you have a small isolated image, cut it out and glue it to a sheet of white paper. Leave extra white space for your child to add ideas.

VARIATIONS

Offer a pencil and eraser for older children.

Put a series of images together and make a story.

Children can be motivated by choice! Offer your child a few images to choose from.

"Charcoal is fun. I didn't know about it before."–Cooper

13 CHARCOAL AND NATURE

- Compressed charcoal
- Kneaded eraser
- Nature objects, such as pine cones and seashells
- Small rag
- Textured paper, such as construction or watercolor

Set up natural objects. Show your child how to draw with the tip and edge of the charcoal to create different effects. Demonstrate how the rag can be used to blend the charcoal and how the kneaded eraser can remove the charcoal. Invite your child to draw.

TIPS

Collect natural objects on a walk with your child, then use them as subjects for charcoal drawing.

If your eraser is new, stretch the eraser apart and knead it into a squishy mass. Form it into a sharp point for small detailed erasing.

Charcoal can be messy, so cover your table if this concerns you. If your child doesn't like the feeling of charcoal, wrap a tissue around the end of it to keep fingers cleaner.

Break it into shorter pieces for small hands.

The arts teach children that problems can have more than one solution and that questions can have more than one answer.

—Elliot Eisner, professor of art and education

PART 2

PAINT, WATER, SPONGES,

AND OTHER WET MATERIALS

(14) CIRCLE STAMPING

- Cups, lids, paper towel tubes, and other round printing objects
- Heavy paper
- Paper plates (two to four)
- Tempera poster paint

Pour a small amount of paint on each paper plate and spread the paint so it's not too thick. Invite your child to dip the objects into the paint and stamp circle shapes on the paper.

VARIATIONS

For younger children, roll out a large sheet of paper and set this up on a low table where the child can easily stand.

Print with dark colors on white paper or light colors on dark paper.

Offer a paintbrush to add details or fill in areas.

Once the paint is dry, add in details with oil pastels, markers, or crayons.

Push this beyond circles and make stamps with other household objects like a potato masher or the bottom of a berry basket.

"I mixed two different colors to make a circle."–Ava

15 SPONGE STAMPER

- Adult scissors
- Clothespins
- Drawing paper or heavy paper
- Paper plates (two to four)
- Sponges
- Tempera poster paint

Pour a small amount of paint on each paper plate and spread the paint so it's not too thick. Cut sponges up into different shapes or sizes. Attach a clothespin to each sponge to act as a handle. Invite your child to pick up the sponges by the clothespins and dip them in the paint to make prints on the paper.

TIPS

If the paint is too thick, add in water to thin it out.

Some children will prefer to dip sponges directly into the paint, without the aid of a clothespin. That's fine! Just be prepared for some handwashing.

VARIATIONS

Use squishy makeup sponges, sea sponges, or bubble wrap for different textures.

Draw with markers first, and then stamp with sponges.

"First I made a tape shape. I decided to paint it on the outside too, because then it's like something tiny is inside it. Using tape is actually pretty cool because you can make super straight lines."–Ty

16 TAPE PAINTING

- Painter's tape
- Small rag
- Water, in jar
- Watercolor paint
- Watercolor paintbrushes
- Watercolor paper

With tape, create shape outlines or lines on the watercolor paper. Set this up alongside paint, a jar of water, a brush, and a rag. Invite your child to paint. When the paint dries, remove the tape for a magical reveal.

TIPS

To clean the brush between colors, demonstrate how to place the brush in the water jar and gently dance the brush up and down to release all the pigment.

If the brush is too wet, demonstrate how the rag can be used to absorb excess water.

VARIATIONS

Invite your child to decide where to add the tape to the paper.

Instead of tape, attach stickers such as coding labels to the paper. Invite your child to paint, and then remove the stickers to reveal white spaces.

"I like using all of the tools in this project."–Carmen

⑰ BLACK-AND-WHITE TEXTURES

- Black tempera poster paint
- Heavy paper
- Paintbrushes
- Paper plates (two)
- Stamping tools, such as a fork, cotton swab, small cup, and straw
- White tempera poster paint

Pour a small amount of white paint on one paper plate and black on the other. Spread the paint so it's not too thick. Set up a variety of stamping tools and paintbrushes alongside the paint and heavy paper. Invite your child to stamp and paint.

VARIATIONS

Try adding black and white paint to black paper or colorful paper. What background does your child prefer? What differences do they notice?

Children may notice that grey is the result of mixing black and white together. Different shades can be achieved by adjusting how much black or white is mixed in. Set up more paper plates and encourage your child to mix various shades to paint with.

When the paint dries, offer your child colorful paint to fill in areas with color.

TIP

Painting with just black and white can help children focus on shape, line, texture, and value (the lightness or darkness of a color).

"I used the stencil brush to make the tree. You can use stickers to hold the stencil down while you paint, and then use colored pencils or markers to color inside of it."–Emeline

18 STENCIL STORIES

- **Heavy paper**
- **Markers**
- **Painter's tape**
- **Paper plate**
- **Stencil brush, dabber, or short scrubby paintbrush**
- **Stencils**
- **Tempera poster paint**

Pour a small amount of paint (color of your choice) on the paper plate and spread the paint so it's not too thick. For a young child, tape a stencil to the paper and invite the child to fill in the shape with paint. For an older child, offer a variety of stencils for them to choose from. Demonstrate how to tape a stencil to paper and stamp paint over the open shape. Invite your child to create a picture or story with the stencils and markers.

TIPS

Use a small amount of paint when stenciling, because a little paint goes a long way. If there's too much paint on the brush, it can go under the stencil for less crisp lines.

Keep the stencil brush vertical to the paper and dab it up and down (if it's a sponge) or move it in small circles (if it's made of stiff bristles).

If you don't have a stencil, draw a design on a paper plate and cut it out with a craft knife.

Encourage your child to experiment with the stencil brushes. What different effects can they create?

VARIATIONS

Move the stencil to different areas of the paper to make a pattern.

Use a variety of stencils to make a scene.

Use fabric paint and stencil a design on a T-shirt or kitchen towel.

"I like painting in a circle shape."–Layla

⒆ PAINTED PLATES

- Paper plates
- Permanent markers
- Rag
- Water, in jar
- Watercolor paint
- Watercolor paintbrushes

Set up a paper plate next to markers, paint, brushes, water, and a rag. Invite your child to draw on the plate, and then add paint over the drawings. Clean the brush with water and the rag between colors.

TIPS

The round plate is a novel material that presents children with the design challenge of filling a circular space. This could encourage circle-inspired designs such as mandalas or pictures created in the center of the plate. Be open to all possibilities.

If your child only uses the paint or just the markers, that's okay!

Something to keep in mind: Markers will dry out if they're used over wet paint.

To clean the brush between colors, demonstrate how to place the brush in the water jar and gently dance the brush up and down to release all the pigment.

If the brush is too wet, demonstrate how the rag can be used to absorb excess water.

VARIATIONS

Set up plates with poster paint for thicker, less detailed designs.

Set up plates with just markers (no paint) for a drawing prompt.

Set up the plates with just paint, and after they dry, offer permanent markers for the details.

"I'm painting a lemon! Since the lemon is smooth there's a
circle around it. The grapes are dots so there are dots
around them. There are wiggly lines around the lettuce
because it's really crazy, like my hair!"–Hadley

20 LARGE-SCALE CIRCLE PAINTING

- Containers to hold paint
- Large sheet of paper
- Painter's tape
- Sturdy paintbrushes
- Tempera poster paint
- Watercolor paintbrushes

Cover a table with a large sheet of paper or pieces of paper that are taped together. You can also tape the paper down so it won't wiggle. Fill containers with different colors of paint. Water the paint down if it's too thick. Add a watercolor paintbrush and a sturdy paintbrush to each container. If you have more than one child, consider adding additional brushes. Start the painting off with a few circles that act as prompts to get ideas flowing. Invite your child to paint.

TIPS

Due to its scale, this is a fun and easy project to collaborate on. As you work, you can comment on your ideas or how you're experimenting.

Mix each of the tempera poster paints with a little bit of white to create pastels.

VARIATIONS

Limit the paint colors to a color family for unity.

Instead of circles, paint a few lines (wavy, zigzag, horizontal) or different shapes.

Offer blank paper without pre-painting any additional prompts.

Tape the paper to a fence or outdoor wall for vertical painting.

TINKERLAB ART STARTS

㉑ DOT PAINTING

- Containers to hold paint
- Cotton swabs
- Liquid watercolor or food coloring
- Watercolor paper

Fill containers, such as an ice cube tray or jars, with liquid watercolors. Place one cotton swab in each color. Invite your child to paint. Dotting and spreading the paint are the most popular ways to use the cotton swab brushes, and maybe your child will invent another technique!

TIPS

If you want to use less paint, liquid watercolors or food coloring can be diluted with water.

If the cotton swabs lose their structure, simply replace with fresh ones.

Pointed tip cotton swabs may hold their strength and shape longer than traditional cotton swabs.

VARIATIONS

Offer only black paint to explore contrast against the white paper.

Try this with poster paint for a thicker painting experience.

Offer white and brightly colored poster paint with black paper.

Write your child's name in large letters with pencil and invite your child to follow the lines with dots of paint.

"I like cotton swabs better than a paintbrush. It's not fat. It's skinnier so you can make better details."–Charlotte

㉒ SPREADING COLORS

- **Containers to hold paint**
- **Liquid watercolors or food coloring**
- **Paper towels or coffee filters**
- **Pipette or eyedropper**
- **Tray**

Squeeze liquid watercolors into individual containers. Use containers that are tall enough to hold the pipettes. This prompt can be messy, so cover the table and be sure to use a tray under the work to catch drips. Invite your child to pull the paint into the pipette and release it on the absorbent paper. If children are new to this technique, demonstrate the following: place the pipette in the watercolor container and squeeze the bulb of the pipette. While the pipette is still in the container, release the bulb to bring the paint into it. Once the paint is in the pipette, remove it from the container.

VARIATIONS

Cut coffee filters or paper towels into different shapes.

To work on fine motor skills, invite your child to separate the coffee filters.

Once the paint is dry, create a decorative banner with the colorful papers, string, and tape.

Try this with other absorbent materials such as doilies, cotton rounds, cotton fabric, or paper napkins.

TIP

If you want to use less paint, liquid watercolors or food coloring can be diluted with water (shown here).

"I liked painting it. It just became a dragon! I used
a pipe cleaner to make a tail and eyebrows."-Taisen

㉓ EGG CARTON PAINTING

- Cardboard egg carton
- Paintbrush
- Rag
- Tempera cake paint or tempera poster paint
- Treasures, such as pom-poms, beads, and buttons
- Water, in jar
- White glue

Cut off the bottom of the egg carton, place it on the worktable, and surround it with paint supplies. Invite your child to paint the egg carton. Once the paint is dry, invite your child to embellish the carton with treasures and glue.

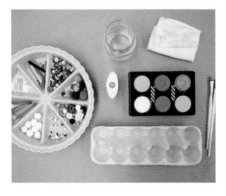

TIP

If your child has other ideas, such as cutting and adding pipe cleaners to their work or painting the inside of the egg carton, be open to these possibilities.

VARIATIONS

Paint the entire egg carton (top and bottom—don't cut off the bottom). When dry, use the carton to store treasures.

Depending on the design of your egg carton, you could cut out a group of four egg holders in a square to make a flower shape (glue a pom-pom in the middle).

Cut the carton into a group of six in a row to make an insect (add eye stickers and chenille stem antennae).

Paint the egg carton with tempera poster paint.

After painting, offer your child scissors, paper, and glue to add embellishments.

TINKERLAB ART STARTS

(24) SQUEEZE AND SCRAPE

- Heavy paper
- Old credit cards, small pieces of cardboard, fork, and/or combs
- Tempera poster paint

Squeeze dots of paint onto a sheet of paper and invite your child to spread the paint with credit cards, cardboard, a fork, and/or combs.

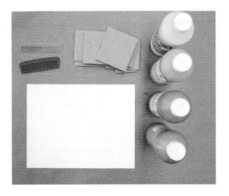

VARIATIONS

Invite your child to independently squeeze dots of paint onto the paper and scrape it across. (Note: this can easily turn into more squeezing and less scraping!)

Make wrapping paper: Roll out a large sheet of paper and cover it with scraped painting.

Squeeze a thin layer of black paint (or color your choice) on a paper plate. Invite your child to dip the edge of the cardboard or credit card in the paint and then stamp paint lines on the paper.

TIP

This can quickly turn into finger painting—be open to this possibility, and be ready with a wet rag.

"It's helpful to have multiple colors for the dots. The cardboard texture really shows up. The way she was using her fingers and hands took it in new directions."—Angela (parent)

"I think this is interesting because you can stick things on the glue, and these are the three primary colors so you can make any color with the glue."—Madeline

㉕ GLUE PAINTING

- **Heavy paper**
- **Liquid watercolors or food coloring**
- **Skewer or other wood stick**
- **Small glue bottles**
- **Treasures, such as sequins, feathers, and buttons**

Open the glue bottles and squeeze in a few drops of liquid watercolors or food coloring. Evenly mix the paint into the glue with a skewer and recap the bottles. Set up the glue bottles next to heavy paper and treasures. Invite your child to squeeze the glue onto the paper to make designs, then attach small treasures to the glue.

TIPS

If you're concerned about a mess, place the paper inside a tray to contain glue drips.

Allow the glue to dry completely before turning the paper vertical.

VARIATION

Make a hanging banner: Draw glue designs on white muslin fabric. When dry, attach one edge of the fabric to a twig with hot glue. Glue a ribbon loop to the back of the twig and hang your creation on a wall.

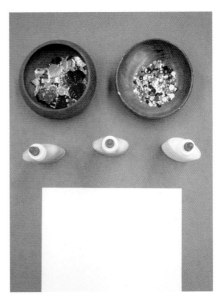

"All of these projects don't have a specific goal in mind, so she was able to enjoy the process."–Karina (parent)

 26 BLEEDING TISSUE PAPER

- **Bleeding tissue paper (small pieces)**
- **Water, in jar**
- **Watercolor paintbrush**
- **Watercolor paper**

Set up your workspace with watercolor paper, a water jar, a paintbrush, and tissue paper. This invitation to create can benefit from a short demonstration: Paint a small amount of water on the paper and place a piece of tissue paper on top of the water. Allow the tissue paper to sit there for a few seconds and then remove it to reveal a colorful mark. Discuss what they think happened. Invite your child to experiment with the tissue paper and water.

TIP

Ask your child what they think could happen if two colors of tissue paper overlap on the paper.

VARIATIONS

When the paper dries, offer permanent markers and invite your child to add images on top of the colorful background.

Explore patterns by inviting your child to alternate colors in a grid, circle, or line.

Children need what
we rarely give them
in school—time for
messing about.

—John Holt, author and
educator

PART 3

PAPER SCRAPS, FELT, GLUE,

AND OTHER COLLAGE MATERIALS

"This is super simple and won't be hard to replicate. I never would have thought of using contact paper for art making. I like the flexibility of this prompt because they can play with it for a while."-Brittany (parent)

27 CONTACT PAPER AND TREASURES

- Adult scissors
- Child scissors
- Clear vinyl contact paper
- Painter's tape
- Yarn

Tape the corners of a sheet of clear contact paper, sticky-side up, to the table. Precut assorted yarn colors, cut into 4- to 10-inch (10- to 25-centimeter) pieces. Place the yarn and child scissors next to the contact paper. Invite your child to create a composition by attaching the yarn to the contact paper. Children can use the scissors to cut the yarn into smaller pieces. When the work is done, you can save it by covering it with another piece of contact paper, sticky sides facing each other.

VARIATIONS

Draw lines on a sheet of drawing paper, place this beneath the clear contact paper, and invite your child to follow the lines with the yarn.

If you don't have contact paper, paint a thin layer of white glue over a piece of heavy paper and invite your child to attach the yarn to the sticky paper.

"This is a heart sprinkle cookie that me and my
sister share with chocolate milk and juice. I
like that there were so many fun things we could
choose from."-Elizabeth

28 COLOR FAMILY COLLAGE

- Cardboard or wood base
- Child scissors
- Containers to hold materials
- Glue, in jar

- Paper scraps, stickers, and treasures from the same color family
- Sturdy paintbrush

Place a brush in the glue. Set up your space with a cardboard or wood base, a glue jar, scissors, paper scraps, and treasures. Invite your child to create a collage with the materials. This project works well with layers of materials. See the variations for several layering ideas.

TIPS

Tailor the colors of this invitation to the season or to your child's interests.

It's okay if your child wants to add materials or paint from other color families.

VARIATIONS

Have a color hunt and invite your child to help you collect the supplies.

Preceding this project, have a painting party with paint colors from your color family. When the paint dries, collage on top of the painting.

Start a collection of old painting projects, and create an assortment of painted papers from this collection that are ready to cut up for collages.

When the collage is complete, draw on top of it with a permanent marker or tempera paint sticks.

TINKERLAB ART STARTS

29 EPHEMERAL FELT SHAPES

- Colored felt
- Large piece of white felt, roughly 12 x 18 inches (30 x 46 centimeters)
- Sharp scissors (adult use only)

Precut the colored felt into different sized shapes such as circles, rectangles, and semicircles. Place the large sheet of white felt in the work area and position the small shape pieces around it. Invite your child to create a felt shape composition on the large white felt background. The collage is ephemeral, meaning it's impermanent. When the image is complete, remove the colored pieces off the white felt and start again.

TIPS

Visually suggest how to use the materials by seeding the white piece of felt with 5–8 arranged shapes, or set up another large piece of white felt for yourself to experiment with.

Images can be abstract or realistic.

Take a picture if you'd like to save a memory of the creation.

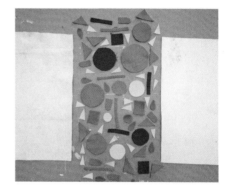

VARIATIONS

Work within a color family and offer seasonal shapes and colors.

Try different background colors (dark blue could indicate a night sky, for example).

Offer a challenge to create something specific from a lesson or recent experience such as a mandala, vehicle, nature scene, or house.

"I'm going to put some pollen in. Look at my tree! I'm working so hard. I'm going to use all these circles. I'm making this beautiful."–Carolyn

30 GEOMETRIC PAPER SHAPES

- Adult scissors
- Construction paper
- Easel paintbrush
- Glue, in jar
- Heavy paper
- Markers

Precut the construction paper into geometric shapes such as rectangles, squares, circles, and triangles. Place the glue jar with brush next to the heavy paper, construction paper pieces, and markers. Invite your child to make a picture with the markers, paper, and glue.

TIPS

Older children may enjoy having a pair of child scissors to further cut the shapes.

Paper can be torn to make new shapes.

VARIATIONS

Offer paper in a seasonal color family.

Punch out circles with a large hole puncher (also a fun fine motor activity for kids).

"I cut out stars. I drew the shapes and then I cut out the shapes. I was making a pattern."–Genevieve

㉛ TISSUE PAPER COLLAGE

- Child scissors
- Glue, in jar
- Permanent markers
- Sturdy paintbrush
- Tissue paper
- Watercolor paper

Precut or tear tissue paper into small and large pieces. Set up the workspace with tissue paper, child scissors, glue (with paintbrush), watercolor paper, and permanent markers. Invite your child to draw on the paper, then paint glue on the paper and gently lay the tissue paper on top. Demonstrate how to layer the paper to create new colors.

TIPS

Children who are unable to use scissors can participate in this activity by tearing the paper or using precut pieces of paper.

Permanent markers work well for this project because their marks won't bleed when wet glue touches them. If you don't have permanent markers, use crayons, colored pencil, tempera paint sticks, or oil pastels.

VARIATIONS

For a shiny background, tape a large piece of foil to the workspace. Invite your child to glue tissue paper to the foil.

Offer permanent markers so your child can draw on top of the dry collage.

Offer stickers, sequins and glue, or paint so your child can decorate on top of the dry collage.

32 COLLAGE BUFFET

- Assorted collage materials: scrap paper and treasures
- Bowls
- Cardboard, or other sturdy base
- Child scissors
- Glue, in jar
- Markers
- Scissors
- Sturdy paintbrush

Fill bowls with assorted collage materials, such as stickers, beads, buttons, and scrap paper. Place a paintbrush in the glue jar. Set up these supplies alongside the base material, markers, and scissors. Invite your child to add collage supplies to the base with glue and to draw with markers.

TIP

Children are often captivated by new materials, so repeating this project with a different selection of supplies can be highly successful.

VARIATIONS

When the collage is dry, offer paint or oil pastels for another layer.

Before getting started, make a border around the base with paint or decorative tape.

Make this seasonal with natural objects such as leaves or seashells.

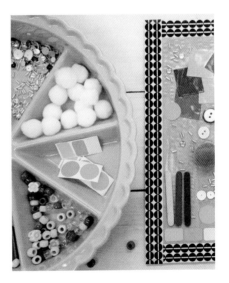

TINKERLAB ART STARTS

③ PAPER PUNCHING

- **Assorted paper punchers**
- **Copy paper or origami paper**

Set up one or more paper punchers next to the paper. Invite your child to punch holes from paper.

TIP

Large "squeeze punch" hole punchers are easy for small hands to squeeze.

VARIATIONS

Once you have a selection of punch-outs, bring out the glue and a sheet of paper and make a collage. Make a pattern with the punch-outs.

With string and tape or stickers, turn the punch-outs into a festive garland.

Invite your child to punch holes around a piece of cardstock or a paper plate, and then offer yarn and a darning needle (a large, blunt needle) to sew through the holes (see Simple Sewing, page 143).

# **34 FABRIC COLLAGE**

- Cardboard or other sturdy base
- Fabric scraps
- Glue, in jar
- Sturdy paintbrush

Precut the fabric into various shapes and sizes. Invite your child to make a composition by placing the fabric on the cardboard. Fabric can be attached with a paintbrush and white glue.

VARIATIONS

Offer ribbon strips, pom-poms, and/or beads alongside the fabric.

Cut fabric into representational shapes, such as flower petals or clouds.

Offer markers to first draw on the base, and then add fabric pieces on top.

Offer inspiration and structure by cutting a paper base shaped like a heart, egg, tree, house, rainbow, or name initial.

TINKERLAB ART STARTS

35 BLACK SHAPES AND GLUE

- **Black construction paper**
- **Glue, in jar or glue stick**
- **Sturdy paintbrush**
- **White paper**

Precut black construction paper into various shapes, such as squares, triangles, and circles. Set up black paper shapes alongside white paper, glue, and paintbrush. Invite your child to create a composition. Paper shapes can be attached with white glue and a paintbrush or with a glue stick.

VARIATIONS

To extend this project, offer tempera or gel crayons and invite your child to draw around the shape composition.

Reverse the collage with white paper scraps on black paper

Offer your child white chalk or a white oil pastel to draw around or on the collage.

"I'm putting circles on top of the circle.
That will be really hard to glue."-Aria

36 DOT AND CIRCLE COLLAGE

- Circle stickers
- Dot (bingo) markers
- Drawing or heavy paper
- Glue, in jar
- Hole punchers
- Markers
- Origami or colored copy paper
- Sturdy paintbrush

Set up a variety of materials for making circles. Invite your child to create a composition with circles as the starting point.

TIPS

If your child is new to using a hole punch, start with Paper Punching (page 113) or demonstrate how it works.

Circle stickers can be found in the office supply section in supermarkets.

VARIATIONS

Cut or punch holes into the paper, and then invite your child to draw around the holes.

Combine this with other circle prompts in this book, such as Circle Drawings (page 51) or Dot Painting (page 87).

TINKERLAB ART STARTS

37 ABSTRACT SHAPE COLLAGE

- Adult scissors
- Construction paper
- Glue, in jar, or glue stick
- Sturdy paintbrush
- White paper

Precut paper into a variety of shapes—circles, semicircles, arrows, ovals, triangles, and abstract blobs. Invite your child to create a composition on the white paper. Paper shapes can be attached with white glue and a paintbrush or with a glue stick.

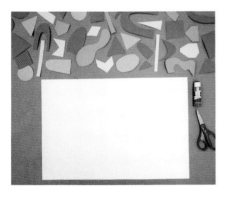

VARIATIONS

Offer oil pastels or gel crayons and invite your child to embellish the collage by drawing details or coloring areas in.

Offer child scissors to children who would enjoy cutting their own shapes.

As an alternative to usual white paper, offer colorful or dark paper for the background.

TIP

To save time cutting, cut shapes from a stack of three to four papers.

38 BUTTONS AND GLUE

- Buttons
- Glue, in jar
- Heavy paper
- Sturdy paintbrush

Fill a small bowl with buttons. No buttons? Beads, large sequins, and macaroni also work. Paint dots of glue on the paper and invite your child to attach buttons to the glue dots.

TIP

Don't leave young children unattended with small objects like buttons, which can easily find their way into mouths, ears, and noses.

VARIATIONS

If your child is learning how to use a glue bottle, replace the jar of glue with a glue bottle. This is an excellent prompt for experimenting with glue squeezing.

For toddlers, pre-squeeze dots of glue all over the paper and invite the child to attach the buttons to the glue.

39 STICKERS AND CRAYONS

- Crayons
- Painter's tape
- Small rag
- Stickers
- Water, in jar
- Watercolor paint
- Watercolor paintbrush
- Watercolor paper

Tape a border around the edges of the paper. Set up stickers and crayons. Invite your child to attach stickers to the paper and draw. When this seems to run its course, introduce watercolors and invite your child to paint. Once dry, the tape can be removed to reveal a border.

TIPS

Inexpensive stickers such as coding labels are wonderful for this project.

If children are new to stickers, they'll likely be excited about this fresh material. Be prepared for them to use a *lot* of stickers.

VARIATIONS

Replace crayons with oil pastels or gel crayons.

On your own paper, demonstrate how stickers can be removed once the paint dries to reveal white paper underneath.

Children who enjoy peeling and attaching stickers may also enjoy peeling and attaching tape in Crayons and Tape (page 47).

Failure is instructive. The person who really thinks learns quite as much from his failures as from his successes.

—John Dewey, psychologist and educator

PART 4

BLOCKS, BEADS, TOOTH-PICKS,

AND OTHER BUILDING MATERIALS

TINKERLAB ART STARTS

⑳ BLOCKS AND POM-POMS

- **Blocks**
- **Craft sticks**
- **Pom-poms**

Set up the blocks, craft sticks, and pom-poms. Invite your child to build with the materials.

VARIATIONS

Encourage your child with a design challenge such as "build a tall structure," or "create a tunnel," or "make a symmetrical structure" with these materials.

Try balancing and building with rocks, pebbles, and small bricks to make towers, homes, and other structures.

Bring other small toys or action figures to the scene to encourage imaginative play.

TIPS

This prompt often leads to imaginative play and elaborate structure building.

It's okay if your child doesn't use all of the materials or chooses to bring other materials into the building activity.

"That's Venice and these are undersea cables. These are the backup cables. This is Italy, and this is London." —Nirvan

ⓐ PLAYDOUGH AND LOOSE PARTS

- Beads
- Buttons
- Craft sticks
- Playdough (see page 157)
- Straw pieces
- Toothpicks

Set this up on a smooth surface. Roll the playdough into balls. Demonstrate how dough can be flattened, how small pieces of dough can connect with toothpicks or crafts sticks, and how texture can be added to the dough by stamping it with the loose parts. Invite your child to build with the playdough and loose parts.

VARIATIONS

Relate this to your child's interests or recent explorations by inviting your child to create a story that connects to a school theme, family trip, or holiday.

Offer loose parts from the pantry such as dry pasta, lentils, and beans, and invite your child to add them to the playdough.

TIPS

Playdough will stick to carpets, so set this up over an uncarpeted floor.

Playdough can be stored in an airtight container and reused another day.

42 PLAYDOUGH STAMPING

- Playdough (see page 157)
- Rolling pin
- Stamping tools, such as forks, jar lids, or a potato masher

Set this up on a smooth surface. Offer your child a mound of playdough and demonstrate how to roll it out with a rolling pin. This alone could be an afternoon of fun. Once it's rolled flat, invite your child to make textures and marks in the dough with stamping tools.

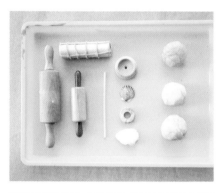

VARIATIONS

Roll more than one color of playdough together for an ombré, marbled, or rainbow effect.

Offer natural materials for stamping—pine cones, seashells, and twigs, for example—with natural-colored dough.

Mix dried lavender flowers or cinnamon into the clay to scent it.

TIP

If you're looking for smooth surface ideas, try using a cookie sheet, laminated place mat, vinyl tablecloth, or glass tabletop.

"I'm making a cake with flower cookies on
the side, and sprinkles."–Reese

㊸ PLAYDOUGH BAKERY

- **Baking tray**
- **Cookie cutters**
- **Muffin tin**
- **Playdough (see page 157)**
- **Rolling pin**

Set this up on a smooth surface. Offer your child a mound of playdough and demonstrate how to roll it flat with a rolling pin. Cut a "cookie" from the dough. Invite your child to make cookies, muffins, and cakes.

VARIATIONS

Offer skewers and toothpicks for building elevated, multilevel cakes.

Offer other baking tools, such as a small pie tin or pie crimper.

Make bakery signs and open up a pretend shop from a nicely covered table or oversized cardboard box. Set up a cake platter for your baker to show off their masterpieces.

Offer birthday candles, sequins, beans, dry pasta, or lentils to decorate the desserts.

Provide various colors of playdough to make rainbow cakes.

TIP

If you offer more than one color of dough, children may want to mix colors. If this happens, try not to stop them. If you don't want your colors to mix, offer just one color.

"Look, it's an alien! His name is Cutie. It has a
lot of eyes and a lot of stuff sticking out of him.
The playdough is fun!"–Theodore

(44) MIXED-MEDIA MODELING CLAY SCULPTURES

- Beads
- Craft sticks
- Modeling clay
- Thin wire or pipe cleaner pieces
- Toothpicks
- Wire cutter (adult use)

Roll a ball of modeling clay and set it up alongside beads, sticks, and wire. Demonstrate how the wire can poke into and attach to the clay, and then how the beads can slip onto the wire. Invite your child to build with these supplies.

TIPS

If you feel like your child is ready to use the wire cutter, demonstrate how to safely use the tool.

Ask, "I wonder how you could bend the wire?"

VARIATIONS

Encourage storytelling.

No modeling clay? Try this with a playdough base.

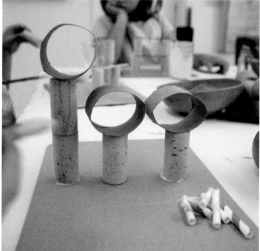

TINKERLAB ART STARTS

45 CARDBOARD CIRCLES AND CRAFT STICKS

- Adult scissors
- Cardboard, or other sturdy base
- Corks
- Craft sticks
- Glue, in jar
- Paper straws
- Paper towel tubes
- Sturdy paintbrush

Precut the straws and paper towel tubes into shorter pieces. Set up the paper towel pieces, cardboard base, craft sticks, corks, straws, glue, and the sturdy paintbrush. Invite your child to build a sculpture with these materials.

VARIATIONS

Once the glue is dry, paint the sculpture with poster paint or liquid watercolors.

Embellish with yarn, feathers, or other treasures.

Paint the cardboard circles and craft sticks *before* assembling the pieces together with glue. Allow them to dry before building with them.

TIPS

Ask, "I wonder what you could build with these supplies?"

If your child wants to add other materials such as yarn, be open to this possibility.

TINKERLAB ART STARTS

46 STRINGING BEADS

- Adult scissors
- Beads with large holes
- Darning needle or other blunt needle with a large eye
- Yarn or thin wire

Cut a piece of yarn to about 24 inches (61 centimeters). Double thread the needle by pulling the yarn through the eye and tying the two ends together into a knot that's bigger than the bead holes. Pour beads into a bowl. Invite your child to string the beads onto the yarn. For a bracelet or necklace, leave a little bit of a tail, cut the yarn from the needle, and tie the two ends together.

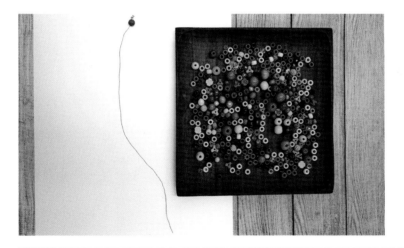

VARIATIONS

If you use wire, make a spiral or loop at one end to secure the beads as they slip onto the wire.

Use unpainted wooden beads and paint them either before or after stringing them on the yarn.

(47) SIMPLE SEWING

- Adult scissors
- Burlap or other large-weave fabric
- Darning needle or other blunt needle with a large eye
- Embroidery hoop
- Yarn

Cut a piece of yarn about 36 inches (91 centimeters) long. Double thread the needle by pulling the yarn through the eye and tying the two ends together into a knot. Cut a square of fabric that's at least three inches larger than the embroidery hoop on all sides. Separate the hoop into two pieces. Place the smaller hoop under the fabric and place the larger hoop on top of the fabric. Gently squeeze them together so that they catch the fabric in the hoop. Tighten the hoop so it doesn't wiggle. Demonstrate how to push the needle up through the back of the hoop and pull the thread until it stops at the knot. Push the needle back down through the top to the back and keep repeating until there's about a 3-inch (8 centimeter) tail. Add more yarn if you want to keep going.

TIP

Young children will naturally wrap their stitches around the frame. You can gently suggest otherwise, or simply allow them to go with it.

VARIATIONS

Try this with embroidery floss.

Add beads or buttons as you go.

If you don't have an embroidery hoop, you can improvise by cutting a hole from a piece of cardboard. Staple the fabric directly to the cardboard frame.

TINKERLAB ART STARTS

 48 WOOD SCULPTURE

- Cardboard, or other sturdy base
- Glue, in jar
- Sturdy paintbrush
- Wood pieces

Place wood beads, cardboard, and a glue jar with brush on the workspace. Invite your child to attach pieces to the base with glue.

TIPS

You can find small wood pieces at craft stores, and you may even be able to get free cast-off pieces from your local lumber store.

This is an exercise in balance. To create a stable structure, discuss which pieces could be placed first and make guesses about how many pieces could be placed before the structure loses its integrity.

Leave room for your child to add other materials such as craft sticks or pom-poms.

VARIATIONS

When the sculpture is dry, paint it with watercolors or tempera poster paint.

Invite your child to build a city or a tall structure (that won't tip over).

Glue on other loose parts, such as buttons or seashells.

"If you use a thin disk of clay, this could be cool to hang on the wall or turn it into an ornament. You could also incorporate nature, such as dry leaves, twigs, and shells."–Angela (parent)

㊾ CLAY AND BEADS

- Air-dry clay
- Beads, buttons, and other small loose parts
- Paper plate
- Rolling pin
- Water, in bowl

Roll clay into a ball and then flatten it into a disk with a rolling pin. Place the clay on the table alongside a small bowl of water (helpful for smoothing dry clay) and loose parts. Invite your child to press loose parts into the clay. These pieces can be pressed in firmly or they can be used as texture-making tools and then removed. Store drying work on a paper plate.

TIP

Don't worry if your child isn't interested in attaching pieces to the clay. Many children enjoy the feeling of clay, and this activity could become a purely sensory experience of squishing and forming clay.

VARIATIONS

Poke a hole in the clay. After the clay dries, tie a ribbon through the hole for hanging.

When the clay is dry, paint it with acrylic paint or seal it with clear acrylic medium.

"Use thicker paint, like tempera poster paint, for more vivid colors."
-Angela (parent)

⑤⓪ PAINTED BEAD FLOWERPOT

- **Air-dry clay or modeling clay**
- **Plain wood beads**
- **Skewers**
- **Small flowerpot**
- **Tempera cake paint**
- **Water, in jar**
- **Watercolor paintbrushes**

Roll the clay into a ball and press it into the flowerpot so that it fills it about ¾ full. Set up the flowerpot next to beads, paint, brushes, and water. Invite your child to paint the beads and build a "plant" of colored wood beads by threading the beads on skewers and inserting them into the pot.

VARIATIONS

Press real twigs into the clay.

Glue sequins to the wooden beads for extra sparkle.

Paint the flowerpot and/or beads with tempera poster paint.

TIPS

Offer a small rag (not shown here) to dry the brush after cleaning it.

Take inspiration from real flowers before getting started. Talk about the colors, patterns, and textures you notice.

(51) CARDBOARD STRUCTURES

- Child scissors
- Decorative tape
- Low-temperature glue gun
- Small cardboard boxes and/or paper towel tubes
- Tempera paint sticks

Set up cardboard boxes and tubes alongside tape, scissors, paint sticks, and a low-temperature glue gun. Invite your child to build with these supplies. The paint sticks can be used to add decoration or details.

TIP

Low-temperature glue guns are useful because they help bring structures together quickly and securely. These glue guns include built-in cool tips that won't burn small hands, and young children can learn to safely use them independently. Children can be taught to use *hot* glue guns safely by watching you demonstrate how not to touch the hot tip or the freshly squeezed (hot) glue.

VARIATIONS

Offer additional recycled items, such as berry baskets and cardboard pieces.

This prompt leaves a lot of room for imagination. Be open to the possibility of adding treasures such as ribbon, stickers, or paper.

"I'm just weaving!"—Hadley

52 YARN-WRAPPED TWIGS

- Beads
- Child scissors
- Twigs
- Yarn

Form the twigs into a shape and then hold in place by twisting yarn around the connecting spots and knotting in place. Set the twig shapes up next to child scissors, beads, and yarn. Demonstrate how the yarn can be wrapped around the twigs and how yarn can go through the beads. Offer the twig shapes and invite your child to wrap the twigs with yarn. To change colors, cut the yarn and either wrap the tail into the yarn or tie it to a new color. Small children may need help with this step.

VARIATIONS

Connect the twigs with wire instead of yarn.

No twigs? Make frames from chopsticks or skewers. Be sure to cut the sharp end off the skewers.

Attach pom-poms to the design with glue or by tying them on.

Crisscross four twigs at the center and secure with wire to make a snowflake or spiderweb form. Invite your child to wrap yarn around this form.

RESOURCES

FAVORITE SUPPLIES

PENS

Crayola Washable Markers: They're dependable and the colors are vivid. Broad Line (thick) and Super Tips (thin).

COLORED PENCILS

Lyra Ferby Giant Triangular Colored Pencils: The short length and triangular shape make these pencils excellent for small hands.

Prismacolor Premier Colored Pencils: I've been using these for years and years. They're smooth, soft, and rich with color; pencils that will grow with your child.

CRAYONS

Crayola Crayons: This trustworthy brand doesn't disappoint, and the crayons come in every color imaginable.

NOYO Gel Crayons and U.S. Art Supply Super Crayons: Gel crayons didn't exist when I was a kid. If that weren't the case, I'm pretty sure they would have been one of my favorite art supplies because of how versatile they are. I have yet to find a washable gel crayon, so keep this in mind and use them in areas that can withstand a mess. The texture reminds me of lipstick: creamy and smooth. They twist like a glue stick to release more crayon. The pigment is water soluble, so you can blend them with a paintbrush and water.

PASTELS AND CHARCOAL

Chalk Pastels: Mungyo Pastels and Artist's Loft Soft Pastels

Charcoal: General's Compressed Charcoal Sticks. These come in a pack of four and can be broken in half for small hands.

Oil Pastels: Pentel Arts Oil Pastels and Sakura Cray-Pas Oil Pastels

PAINT

We use five kinds of paint in this book: liquid tempera (poster paint), watercolor pans, liquid watercolors, tempera paint cakes, and paint sticks.

Liquid Watercolors: Sargent Art Watercolor Magic Liquid Watercolors and Sax Liquid Washable Watercolor Paint. Both are washable (bonus!) and a little goes a long way. Tips: I've never had a bottle that doesn't leak, so store these upright in a plastic bin. The color is concentrated and you can dilute it with water.

Tempera Paint Cakes: Sax Nontoxic Tempera Paint Cakes. These come in primary colors and neon. I like both. They're more opaque than watercolors, and work just the same. Just add water.

Tempera Paint Sticks: Kwik Stix Solid Tempera Paint and Tempera Paint Sticks by Craft Smart. Tempera paint sticks are opaque like paint, draw like an oil pastel or gel crayon, and dry in a matter of seconds. Because of their thickness and opacity, they're useful for creating a decorative layer on top of collage.

Tempera Poster Paint: Crayola Washable Tempera Paint. I like to mix unique colors in sealable jars, and I encourage you to try this.

Watercolor Pans: Artist Loft Watercolor Pan Set and Prang Pan Watercolor Set. Both rich in pigment and affordable.

PAPER

All-Purpose Paper: Tru-Ray Sulphite Heavyweight Construction Paper (78 pound). This is a great all-purpose paper that can be used for drawing, collage, and painting. It's heavier than printer paper, lighter than most watercolor paper, and more durable than typical construction paper. If you're only getting one type of white paper, this is the one. Tru-Ray also comes in multiple colors

Construction Paper: Pacon Construction Paper. I love it for collage projects and just about anything that requires colorful paper.

Paper Roll: Pacon Kraft Wrapping Paper. Great for murals and for table covering. I use the 48-inch roll, cut to fit our tables, with stainless steel tablecloth clamps to hold it down.

Watercolor Paper: Strathmore Paint Pad is a workhorse, inexpensive watercolor paper that's great for painting experiments. My favorite watercolor paper is Canson Watercolor Paper (140 lb.). It's higher quality than the Paint Pad and worth a splurge.

CLAY

There are three kinds of clay in this book: playdough, air-dry clay, and modeling clay.

Clay: Crayola Air-Dry Clay comes in 2.5-pound and 5-pound buckets. It doesn't require baking, dries hard, and you can paint it with tempera paint when it's dry. It feels just like clay, but keep in mind that this is play clay, not meant to last, and it can crack over time.

Modeling Clay: Crayola Modeling Clay stays moist and doesn't dry out.

Playdough: We like to make our own. See page 157 for the recipe.

See page 157 for the recipe.

EXTRA THINGS

Clear Contact Paper: Con-Tact Brand Shelf Adhesive (clear, 18" x 20').

Paint Jars: Ashland Mini Round Jars with Lids. These airtight jars are the best for storing paint or glue.

Pencil Sharpener: X-Acto School Pro Classroom Electric Pencil Sharpener. It's durable—we've had ours for years. Kids can easily sharpen pencils on their own, and the size dial allows you to sharpen fat pencils. Worth the investment.

Punchers: Fiskars Squeeze Punch. This is a fabulous tool for little ones to use independently for paper-punching projects. It comes in different shapes.

Scissors: Fiskars Classic Pointed and Blunt Scissors. They make these left-handed too.

Stickers: Avery Color Coding Labels. For little ones who love peeling stickers from paper, these circular or rectangular stickers come in packs of 300–1000 stickers, making this economical, colorful, and easy. For variety, also look for colorful reinforcement stickers that look like donuts.

Wood Pieces: Pacon Assorted Wood Pieces and Shapes. I find these in an enormous box (18 pounds), great to share with friends.

White Glue: Elmer's Washable School Glue. I like to buy a gallon and use it to fill smaller bottles as they run out.

PLAYDOUGH RECIPE

This recipe makes buttery soft playdough in multiple colors.

2½ cups water
1¼ cup salt
1½ tablespoons cream of tartar
5 tablespoons vegetable oil
2½ cups flour
Liquid watercolors or food coloring

Note: for gluten-free dough, replace the flour with 2 cups rice flour and ½ cup cornstarch.

1. Add the first five ingredients to a large pot and mix. It will be lumpy. Not to worry, the dough will get smoother as it cooks.

2. Cook the dough over a low heat, mixing frequently. The water will slowly cook out of the mixture and you'll notice it starts to take on a sticky dough appearance. Keep mixing until the edges of the dough along the side and bottom of the pot appear dry. This may take a bit of work! Pinch a piece of dough. If it's not gooey, the dough is ready.

3. Remove the dough from the pot and place it on a countertop or large cutting board that can withstand heat and a little food coloring.

4. Knead the warm dough until it's smooth and then divide it into balls that equal the number of colors you'd like to make. Flattening each ball, add a little bit of food coloring or liquid watercolors, and then knead the color in.

5. Play with the dough right away or store it in a large sealable bag or sealed container. Unused, it can keep for months.

TIPS

For natural-colored playdough, leave out the liquid watercolors.

For only one color, add liquid watercolor in step one.

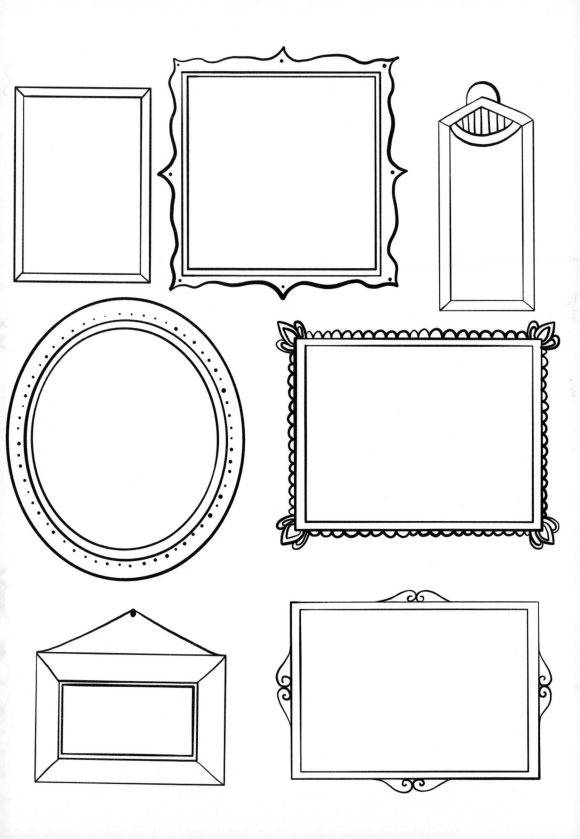

ACKNOWLEDGMENTS

Thank you to Scott, for your love, faith, and encouragement; to Nola and Isla, for being the original TinkerLab project testers; to Erica Silverman, for walking alongside me; to Jenn Brown, for trusting this idea; to Sara Bercholz, for publishing charismatic books that intentionally champion creative human connection; to Audra Figgins for helping this idea grow; to Jessica Hoffman Davis and Elliot Eisner, for encouraging me to think deeply about arts education; to Sister Corita Kent, for showing the world how important it is to notice; to Danielle Ashton, who fills me with friendship and extends my love of art in new directions; to my blogging, teaching, business, and author friends, for inspiring me with your passion and conviction; for my Stanford students, staff, and residents, for bringing your authentic selves to the table and reminding me what it means to shine from the inside; to all of the uplifting children who have come to my art table with a willingness to experiment and play; to my family and friends, for radiating light into my life; and to my mom and dad, for identifying the glow of imagination inside of me and giving it space to shine.

Special thanks to the children in this book for helping me test and invent these invitations to create: Isla, Madeline, Natalie, Anna, Ila, Sasha, Henry, Charlotte, Lucy, Taisen, Pfeifer, Genevieve, Mabelle, Elizabeth, Carolyn, Ava, Kate, Hadley, Makena, Muriel, Mila, Isaiah, Aria, Adeline, Mason, Cooper, Theodore, Lily, Elliott, Annie, Valentina, Juno, Marlo, Samantha, Emeline, Grant, Ford, Anna, Alexa, Sophia, Tate, Reese, Ty, Nirvan, Henry, Elliot, Rosalind, Oliver, Carmen Sofia, Francesco, Lucy, Gabi, Kai, Liliana, and Vivienne.

INDEX

ABOUT THE AUTHOR

Rachelle Doorley is the founder of the creativity website, TinkerLab, where she has been inspiring families to connect with their kids through art for over a decade. She has a background in theater, art education, and creativity, and is the author of several books. A Stanford lecturer and resident fellow in a college dorm, Rachelle has worked in design and art education for over twenty years and holds a BA in theater from UCLA and an EdM in education from Harvard. She works out of a magical studio filled with old books, shelves of paint, and sharp pencils. She's the mother of two and makes a lot of art. You can learn more at TinkerLab.com.